DYING TO LIVE

Running backwards through cancer, Lupus,

and chronic illness

Amy Susan Crohn

DYING TO LIVE: *Running backwards through cancer, Lupus, and chronic illness*

Cover by Graphicz X Designs (http://graphiczxdesigns.zenfolio.com)

Cover background photo ("September Sunset") and author photo by Sherry Vance

United States Copyright 2013©

ISBN: 1482568098

ISBN-13: 9781482568097

Library of Congress Control Number: 2013907358

www.dyingtoliveamy.com

*Names changed.

This book is dedicated to my husband, Will,

and my sons, Daniel and Brett.

Thank you for your unconditional love.

"Adverse childhood psychosocial experiences 'get under the skin' and leave enduring health signatures."

Andrea Danese M.D., Ph.D
Clinical Lecturer in Child & Adolescent Psychiatry
Kings College London, University of London

"The vision must be followed by the venture. It is not enough to stare up the steps – we must step up the stairs."

Vance Havner, theologian, 1901–1986

"Beautifully told, this story of a happy young wife and mother suddenly diagnosed with two usually fatal diseases will inspire all who read it. Alternately loved and abused by her charismatic, disturbed parents, Amy Susan Crohn discovers the causes of her rare condition and fights to reclaim her joyful, loving life. Along the way, she discovers the connection between her childhood abuse and the devastating illnesses. Lessons for us all that may well save our lives someday, this riveting, sensitive and often humorous memoir is an instant classic. "

Laura Shaine Cunningham
Sleeping Arrangements & A Place in the Country

"In this heart-wrenching yet ultimately uplifting memoir, Amy Susan Crohn recounts her journey through childhood neglect and emotional abuse, multiple life-threatening chronic diseases, medical indifference, and near-death experience, to emergence as a fulfilled wife, mother, marketing strategist, author, and child advocate. Moving artfully back and forth in time and space and through fluctuating states of consciousness, she weaves her story with passion but without self-pity, with sensitivity but without sentimentality, and above all with life-affirming humor and faith. It is a tale of trial, torment, and ultimate triumph, rich with inspiration and lessons for us all."

David B. Sachar, M.D., FACP, MACG, AGAF
First Dr. Burrill B. Crohn Professor of Medicine
Master Edicator, Institute for Medical Education
Director Emeritus, Division of Gastroenterology
Icahn School of Medicine at Mount Sinai

FOREWORD

It was a cold, mid-winter Sunday night. The day had passed uneventfully and I was enjoying a quiet day, coasting to completion of my weekend "on-call". Little did I realize that the events which were about to unfold would be among the most dramatic and unforgettable of my medical career.

I received a call from an ICU nurse. Over the years I had developed an implicit trust and confidence in the clinical skills and judgment of the ICU nursing staff. Being on the front lines, they have an uncanny ability to distinguish between the routine and the truly emergent. Most calls from the ICU nurses are of a controlled, routine nature. This was not such a call. The voice I heard was anguished, insistent: "We need you right away."

A young woman (much younger than the usual ICU patient) was brought to the ICU in critical condition and was deteriorating rapidly. The gravity of the situation was clear: the patient was having difficulty breathing, there was severe swelling of her face and neck, and her vital signs were fading. Making matters worse was the alarming realization that we had no idea what was causing the crisis. She was recently diagnosed with both Lupus and Hodgkin's Disease and a surgical biopsy had been completed. How these diseases had led to this precarious situation was not at all obvious.

This scenario is the start of a medical drama which plays out over the following weeks and years. For Amy Crohn it was the middle of an agonizing nightmare which would bring her to the brink and back, revealing an unbending will to survive.

In reliving Amy's journey we witness all facets of the American health care system. We encounter a medical system capable of life-saving interventions, but which can also at times be impersonal and forbidding. We meet the most caring and dedicated health care professionals, and we also encounter those who are indifferent and *detached. This is a compelling story told by a patient sometimes so sick and weak that her observations are reduced to dream-like impressions.*

Through Amy's story we experience all facets of human emotion, the highs and lows of devastating medical illness are interwoven with memories of a troubled childhood, her joy of marriage and parenthood, ultimately the triumph of hope and determination.

Years after that dreadful mid-winter night when our paths first crossed, Amy appeared at my office for a visit. Before me stood a young woman appearing slightly frail and tentative, but her knowing smile reflected the amazing strength of the human spirit.

Arthur Fass, M.D. M.D., FACC, FACP, Director of Medicine, Phelps Memorial Hospital, Sleepy Hollow, New York

TABLE OF CONTENTS

Prologue 10

"Go Live Your Life" 12

Fragments and Outright Fear 16

Shadows, Secrets and Siblings 23

The Camel and the Spider 35

Three Housekeepers and a Cat 52

Leaning on Rubble 59

Bribes and Ladders 63

Intensive Repair 68

The Lean Mean Years 78

Protect and Defend 83

Chemotherapy x18 91

The Doctor Dilemma 96

The Brooklyn Alphabet 100

Hand Wringers, Pity People, and God 113

Blow the House Down 119

"I Hate Your Guts" 126

The Towers Fall and Daddy Dies 135

The Science 141

Epilogue   148

Acknowledgements   150

Author Biography   153

Appendices   155

PROLOGUE

No one expects a traumatic event; nor should we live like Chicken Little and predict sure catastrophe with: *"The sky is falling. The sky is falling."* But what if your personal sky does fall and your life becomes forevermore divided into *Before* and *After*? That's what happened to me and, regardless of the harrowing events I endured, I had to finally amend my ways and fine-tune my life to accommodate its 'new normal' (a phrase that is becoming hackneyed as survivors of trauma are hearing it over and over again from doctors, caregivers, and therapists).

If you rail against acceptance; fight with all your might to return to the way you were *Before*, you will lose. I did get trampled by both Stage IV cancer and a Lupus diagnosis that wreaked absolute hell on me but reaped an ultimate reward – a truly living and loving life. Furthermore, I learned so much about the value of a life well lived that my sheer determination to overcome somehow won the war.

Along the journey, however, I had a deep awakening about how childhood maltreatment can lead to adult physical illness. Even though I was born into a family of medical celebrity (my Great Uncle Burrill B. Crohn discovered Crohn's Disease), in this book I reference studies that are astounding in how they link the events of our earliest years to our later physical health. It required that I do some serious soul searching including revisiting a past I had sealed to uncover and unmask the scared little girl who crumbled under disease at age 36.

In the folk tale Chicken Little you have a choice of two morals depending upon the telling. The 'happy ending' teaches us not to be 'chicken' but to remain courageous no matter what. Alternately, in the tale that ends with the entire town's bird-folk eaten by a shrewd fox who tricks them into his lair for protection, you are warned not to believe everything you are told.

In my opinion, both bravery and doubt are needed during devastating illness or trauma. We must have tenacity by the tons to endure the sheer pain of it all and not be 'chicken.' Yet we also must grow acute awareness and ever-alert antennae for misinformation about what to eat, tests to be administered, medications to take, process advice from every corner or the earth, and how to proceed in baby steps to live among the living and not be tricked by the fox.

It is my sincere hope that your take-away from this tome will be information of nurturance and education and that you will give yourself permission to choose a path towards grace. As I always wish for my sons as they grow, aim to become kind and wise and your life will surely be enriched.

Amy Susan Crohn

"Go Live Your Life"

It was snowing outside as I shepherded my two little boys, in their matching silk Christmas vests, to see "Mr. and Mrs. Santa Claus" at our community holiday event. At the small recreation center in the Village of Ossining, New York, I wandered around smiling and sharing pleasantries with strangers and friends. In their red and green holiday outfits, my sons met the rosy-cheeked, gift-giving pair and ate McDonald's eggs and biscuits. It took all my strength to smile, talk and walk. My shoulders felt weighted, my legs like lead. We walked to the musical accompaniment – "I'm dreaming of a White Christmas, just like the ones I used to know…"

Only I was not dreaming. I was entering the nightmare that was about to rip open the postcard pretty façade of my life. At last, I sat down on the sidelines – somewhat stunned that "normal" life could go on around me while I held such a deep secret. No one knew what I had just learned – that within me, this "normal" looking woman, a huge freak tumor pressed between my heart and lung, and threatened to explode. I was scheduled for surgery in just a few days and as I watched my eager innocent little boys, I wondered "Will I be here next Christmas?"

At the time, I was still trying to absorb the first shock waves. After several years of odd symptoms: Unexplained aches and pains, mouth sores, nausea, extreme fatigue, confusion and, ultimately, a constant cough, fever, and sweats that soaked my sheets, my family doctor of 10 years, "Dr. C," did minimal tests and dismissed the symptoms as female stress. However, I did take the time to look up my symptoms and a mention of auto-immune disorders made my brain hum.

Often, the sick person recognizes the sickness when confronted with the written description. How could my doctor tell me I was well when I knew I could not be? I trusted him but relationships with doctors are precarious arrangements. If you are honest, as I was over a ten-year period, they know nearly every good, bad and embarrassing thing about you. My family doctor called me "his favorite patient" more than once and we had an easy rapport.

Young and eager, Dr. C had joined a thriving practice with a more-established doctor. My first appointment with him was "love at first sight." I knew I would rather see him than the older doctor who had been my regular physician. I had no reason to doubt Dr. C's care and, while I was relatively well, we enjoyed an easy give-and-take. All that changed when I challenged his authority in this particular instance and we argued. Having so few mentors in my life, I was truly crushed by his behavior and further damaged by his denial of my life-threatening symptoms.

In defiance of my loyalty to Dr. C, I went to a rheumatologist even though my doing so made my "dear" family doctor angry. The rheumatologist confirmed my fears. As they shared an office, Dr. C fought with the specialist, and disputed the findings. It was alarming to hear my trusted, long-term doctor argue with his colleague. Dr. C's last words to me were: "You're a normal 36-year-old woman. Go live your life."

Without my knowing it, a tiny spark of primal survival instinct was lit that day and it flared to anger. I defied my once-cherished family doctor and that was the first step I took to save my own life. From that time forth, I always questioned any doctor's diagnosis until I had explored the consequences, done my own research and sought other medical opinions. Had I listened to that first beloved doctor, my life would have been very brief. I wasn't just "working wife and mother syndrome tired," I was in immediate danger of dying.

Although my self-started business was important and gratifying to me, my life's true center was my family, my husband Will, and our two sons, Daniel and Brett. I loved my husband unquestionably but perhaps my maternal instinct to protect my children was even stronger motivation to fight for my life. Not only did I love my boys to the extreme as most mothers do, but they were both especially hard-won children, after my long struggles to have babies – at all.

Daniel, seven, was my miracle boy, conceived after all fertility tests had said I couldn't have a baby. I suffered several miscarriages, then at last, carried full-term and gave birth to my perfect giggling baby boy. I could play with Daniel for hours on the floor – we were inseparable – weren't we? Brett, at three, was even more vulnerable. Brett was our foster child, taken into our arms and home as fully as Daniel, our birth baby. Undersized and diagnosed likely to be retarded, mentally and physically, Brett was, from the first day at home, our "love bug;" he soon caught up in every developmental way. Within 13 months, he was just as bright and playful and even more cuddly and loving than an average three-year-old boy. He bounced on my lap and into my heart.

Brett needed me maybe even more than my big boy. How could I leave these two small children? Yet I knew as I stared at the pre-Christmas tableaux that I did have to leave; but at that moment, I imagined my absence would be brief – more biopsies, tests in the hospital, surgeries, and, perhaps chemotherapy and radiation. And I knew I was at the start of the most perilous journey of my life. The surgery itself would mean potentially cracking open my rib cage to get close to my tumor and further discover the exact nature of my illness.

I watched my boys' fresh scrubbed faces tilt toward Santa as they wished for what? Toys? Games? Trips to the famous Walter's hot dog stand in Mamaroneck, New York? I wished for the chance to see them make these wishes again, next year. When we went home, I barely made it through the usual fun bedtime rituals of getting the boys fed, bathed, "Ta-Ta-Boop" dinosaur story time, and huge hugs and "special spot" kisses goodnight between their eyes on those tiny bridges of their noses. I wished my husband, Will, could be at home more, but he worked as a New York City firefighter and that meant long hours and overnights at the firehouse.

In my zombie-like state that Christmas season, I was grateful when, a few days later, after the brutal surgical biopsy, Will was able to take time off to assume leadership of the boys. I stayed at home, trying to comprehend the devastating findings – two diseases that could kill me: Lupus and Hodgkin's Lymphoma Stage IVB, the most advanced. With this dual diagnosis, I could sense my odds: grim to hopeless. Surely I would die. On a more dispassionate level, I could appreciate the perfect metaphor – the heart pushed toward explosion. The malignant lymphomatous tumor was growing inside my chest to suppress my very life's breath and heartbeat, while at the same time, a deadly river of immunologically-deranged cells ran through my blood. I was sickening unto death with two likely fatal conditions; and, for whatever reasons, I had become my own enemy. My body had turned against itself; I was unwillingly committing, cell by cell.

I sought more medical information in the hope that I might find an answer. Lupus, the mysterious autoimmune disease that can attack every part of the body is more often chronic than deadly — but it is incurable, its course unpredictable. Hodgkin's Lymphoma is considered the "good" lymphoma, more curable than non-Hodgkin's Lymphoma, the disease that claimed the life of Jacqueline Kennedy Onassis. However, Hodgkin's at its highest stage is dire and the "B" refers to vital organ involvement; in my case, the heart and lung.

Moreover, cancer of the lymph system means your entire body must be treated and chemotherapy plus radiation is usually ordered; however, doctors cannot safely direct radiation at the heart. Survival rates for the lower stages of the disease are very, very good; the higher stages, much less so. In 1997, Hodgkins Lymphoma claimed star NBC executive Brandon Tartikoff, despite all his financial resources and otherwise good health, at age 48. What could possibly be the prognosis for someone with both Lupus and Hodgkin's, diseases which would conspire with each other to neutralize all the most powerful cancer fighting weapons? I realized what that meant – that I had two diseases whose treatments could not be tolerated in tandem. Unless a miracle intervened, I was most likely doomed.

In that moment of awareness, how precious life becomes ... my eyes welled with tears just looking at my husband Will's handsome, caring face, my boys' smiles and calls: "Mommy, look what I got from Santa!" "Daddy! Watch me skateboard!"

Fragments and Outright Fear

My husband Will's life was a string of life-and-death emergencies and the deceptive lulls between them; fighting fire when it struck, saving lives, or discovering charred remains after 9/11. Will was a real-life hero, the love of my life, my handsome hunk, my Italian self-made intellectual, beautiful and ripped, salt-tongued and sweet lipped, smart as a whip and most amazing – he was as in love with me as I was with him.

Will and Amy, c1981.

We were an unlikely pair – I was of Jewish heritage from an intellectual family of some renown and Will came from Brooklyn Italian working class stock. But in various ways, we were both emotionally orphaned, and we fit. We faced life curiously on our own from the start by paying for our own wedding. No one gave me away; my father sat there at the ceremony, but I would not allow him an honor he had not earned. I gave myself to Will and in the spirit of that independent wedding we continued our walk through life, united by our respective duties and more in love than ever. We were both exhausted, as working parents everywhere are, and now we faced our greatest challenge. Unknown to us at that time, was how our love would be tested as never before…

The only course of treatment open to me was to shrink and kill the lymphoma tumor with the most toxic chemicals in the cancer

16

arsenal, a regimen called MOPP. The acronym was largely passé in the oncology field since newer treatments had been discovered and utilized. But because of my vital organ involvement, I had to go 'old school' and, as one of the directors of Memorial Sloan Kettering Cancer Treatment Center told me, "Get ready for nine months of torture." I didn't have to be a scientist to understand these toxic drugs could also kill me. Somehow, I would have to summon the strength to resist the "curative" poisons.

It is also a very curious thing to know you have an autoimmune disease, that your own body is your enemy – the enemy within. The first sign of my acknowledgement was that I could not sleep – 'What was going on inside my body this minute?' I wondered in the dark. Were more cells multiplying, flowering like malignant black orchids? The worst of it was I was somehow doing this to myself. Why? How? If my body attacked itself, could I possibly get it to do the reverse and heal?

Understanding the causes, ferreting out what happened that led my cells to self— destruct, was my only road to recovery. In the course of my illness, I discovered not only how to survive but why I had gotten so sick in the first place. As phase one of my battles for my life began with the biopsy surgery and diagnoses on December 16, 1996, I began to keep a record which, with my notes, became this book and my life became forevermore divided.

* * *

January 5, 1997 is such a date. It is snowing, and my husband takes my two young sons ice skating. Curtained off from the world by the falling snow, I stay alone in our home. Outside the bay window is a postcard of white lace flakes against the trees. Inside, I am restricted to the couch or bed because of pain from three knife-like incisions, medicines that make me woozy, and an unstitched hole, healing inside my chest; the biopsy.

I navigate to the couch but, after two hours, my neck hurts and I feel confused. A few days earlier, I had noted my fingers swelling.

The neck pain sharpens, burns, the pain rising to excruciating; 12 on a scale of one to 10. 'Something is wrong,' I realize. 'Something has gone wrong after my surgical biopsy. This is not supposed to happen.' I feel if I wait much longer, I won't even be able to pick up the phone and call for help. Somehow, I do dial a friend. "Help," I whisper. "I don't think I can walk. I am fading fast." Afterwards, I remember only bits and pieces like bugs skittering across a floor, bare remnants of the experience that forever changed my life.

The body speaks its truth to the person inside it; I was in danger and I knew it. I felt a deep decline and I knew I must go to the hospital yet I was not prepared for the speeding van ride – no time to wait for an ambulance – and the snow thickening into menace. The snow descended, heavy, white, unending, no longer beautiful but gray and needling, itself a threat. The wail of police sirens and ambulances, unseen, screamed of other catastrophes nearby. Into this atmosphere, at once blind and oppressive, I was carried between life and death.

The next flash of memory is of a bored male medical attendant: "If she got in the van under her own power, she can get out. No stretcher." Every movement feels as if I am underwater – strained, heavy. 'Doesn't he know? I didn't get into the van. My neighbors' husbands carried me. Why is he making me get in a wheelchair myself?'

Life has its absurdities, always. As I am being triaged in the emergency room, much is made of my name, Crohn. This always happens in a hospital or doctor's office; Crohn is a superstar name in medicine. As I fight to stay conscious, I hear the inevitable question: "Are you related to the famous Dr.Burrill Crohn who discovered "Crohn's Disease"?

"Yes, I am…" but I am too weak to explain the relationship, the history. "That's a severe disease," I hear someone mistakenly thinking I have Crohn's say. "Crohn's Disease is serious – loss of control of bowels, constant fits of diarrhea, chronic extreme weight loss…the sufferers waste away…"Are you having an attack?" 'Not of Crohn's,' I want to say, 'I am just named Crohn – I don't have it! I do

18

not have Crohn's Disease! I am a Crohn! I am related to Dr. Burrill Crohn! BUT…I am having an attack and it is something entirely different and terrible…'

But at this point, I cannot talk, I am going under to the near unconscious place in which I hear but cannot speak and I am gripped by terror. 'What is happening to me?' I think. 'I know I have two terrible diseases but neither would kill me so fast. They both take a while, dire as my prognosis is, no one would have given me days or hours to live. What IS this attack?' From the start, I concentrate – I am inside myself like a tiny embryo of me – perched somewhere on a ledge in my brain, on the very precipice of my consciousness, my need to surface to see Will, to see the boys again…

'Don't give in, don't go under. Hang on…'

Moments later, on a gurney in an emergency room cubicle, I remember saying softly: "My neck hurts," and, just like that, I am 11 years old again on a terror trip to the Bronx when a girlfriend and I took the wrong bus out of Westchester and we landed in an alien Bronx wasteland. The bus driver pulled out and left us standing there, in a shopping center deserted save for a few bums and gang members lurking. I screamed and screamed, "WAIT! WAIT!" after the bus driver. He couldn't hear me then and no one could hear me now.

A nurse, however, IS screaming.

"Tachy! Tachy!! Tachy!!!" I misinterpret and think: 'Why is she yelling that my clothes are tacky, unstylish? What is that beep, whistle and whoosh sound and where is it coming from? Where did my tacky clothes go?' Much later, I would learn she was saying "tachy," short for tachycardia or a heart racing too fast, out of control.

Moving in and out of consciousness I recall fragments of movement, noise and constant strain. Being lifted. Put down on tables. Needles inserted. Tubes pulling. Talk of transfer to another hospital and a helicopter and thinking, 'I'm not getting in any fucking helicopter!'

Snow too heavy. I see the snow from earlier; an opaque sky as if the world itself is descending into a gray-out just like me. Because of the snowstorm, an ambulance arrives instead of the helicopter. The driver argues with my husband. The orange jump-suited man yells at Will: "Stay in the front passenger seat of the ambulance no matter what happens!"

Arrival at trauma center. Dear friend who took me to the first hospital is touching my toes saying: "You'll be okay." I whisper: "No I'm not. I'm dying." Tears and yells as I'm rolled fast – the attendants are running with the stretcher. 'But where are they taking me?' I dip in and out of consciousness.

Then, without warning, I fly out of my body and am up on the ceiling looking down at myself on the table; wondering why everyone is crying, including the beautiful nurse with the long blonde hair and sparkly eyes? Wondering why my husband, Will, is throwing his body on top of mine crying: "NO! NO! Amy, my soul mate!"

I cannot in that surreal instant understand but looking back, I can see that I was having a classic "out-of-body" experience – the sense of going toward the light, the perfect peace that is reported by so many people who came back from the dead. 'Oh God, please,' I think. 'I have to let Will know I'm feeling fine, no pain in this place of light. I have to get back to Will because when he was just five years old, his mother died at age 36, the same age I am today. I've got to get back to Will and tell him everything is going to be okay.'

My ears fill with pressure and I hear a deep, droning sound as I squeeze through some sort of tunnel. I find I am back on the table, no longer looking down on this death scene. I speak in a soft voice to Will who is holding my hand tight: "I love you. It's going to be alright. I'm not in pain anymore. Say good bye to Daniel and Brett for me." Then I catch myself and draw in my breath – 'Say goodbye to my children?' For an instant, I see the faces of my son, Daniel, seven, and the toddler, Brett, three. 'Say good bye to them? What am I thinking?'

'How could I abandon these little children to a motherless fate? How could I give them this grief?' But I seem to have already departed my physical body – I am again floating high along the ceiling of the ER. I can gaze down. I see my body on the gurney, the figures of my husband and the manic doctors, attendants and nurses around me. Even ethereal, I stiffen with resolve: 'I am NOT leaving quite so fast! No matter how radiant the afterlife, I am not floating off to the next world while I have these two little children in this world. I am not leaving Will, my soul-mate destined to be with me for a long and loving life. I want to outwit the demons. I must survive.'

Sometime later, I awoke in a bright, trauma center intensive care unit. My eyes felt as if they were nailed shut and I couldn't speak. I moved ever so slightly and heard the clink, jingle, clank of many tubes and wires. Frightened, I listened to the whoosh, whoosh, whoosh sound, the beeps and ooze of suction, thumps of God-knows-what. I strain to hear voices. There was a male voice above me, at my left side. Whoever belonged to the voice, gave me a few gentle pats on my arm. There was also a female moving around and around me. I heard her complain: "My shift is over but now I'm stuck with this crummy patient."

My eyes were so dry. I gestured with leaded hands to my eyes. Female voice yelled: "What? What do you want?" I tried again to speak, but no sound came out. Frantic, I again raised my heavy hands to my eyes. I heard the jingle jangle of all the tubes and wires. Female voice snapped again. "I'll be with you in a minute."

It was difficult, but I lifted my right hand and gave her the classic middle finger. Then she knelt next to my ear and said: "Listen, kiddo, if you want anyone to treat you right, you better not have that kind of attitude." Female voice, ranting, left the room. I heard the male push out his chair. Nearly silent, I heard him move with light steps through the room. A few moments later, cool compresses were placed on my eyes. I felt immediate relief and slipped back into unconsciousness.

Waking again, I felt on fire. I heard familiar voices this time – my oldest sister and brother; my husband. I was relieved and then horrified as I heard them discussing my condition. "She looks like the Elephant Man," said my sister. "Why is she so swollen?" asked my brother. I heard my husband's voice crack as he describes bits and details that I still couldn't process. As a New York City firefighter, Will was accustomed to catastrophe but he couldn't keep control as he described my condition. "It's the Lupus," he said. "They call it acute angio-edema due to her immune system reacting against the growing cancer."

Inwardly, I gasped as he continued: "They had to do an emergency tracheotomy. When we got here, the doctor said she only had a pinhole left to breathe." I gestured wildly and they responded, saying my name, laying hands on me wherever there wasn't a tube or wire, telling me: "You will be okay. You will be alright."

I didn't believe them.

I shook my left hand to let them know I wanted to write something down on paper. My eyes were still sealed shut but I had to tell them about that first nurse. My brother gave me pen and paper and, blind, I scribbled something. I worried that my lefty handwriting wasn't good enough.

I made my point because within 10 minutes an administrator was in the room. She apologized about "kiddo" nurse's behavior and I was assigned another nurse. My brother said he was so proud of me. He held my hand while my husband tended to the paperwork; the business of being critically ill in a hospital. I settled back into a kind of dreamland. 'I want my Daddy,' I tried to mouth. 'I want my Daddy.'

Shadows, Secrets and Siblings

From somewhere far away and long ago, I heard my father's sing-song special call to me as a child: 'Amy Sue, where are you?' Why, I wondered before I slid under into unconsciousness, would I hear my father now? But I did. 'Amy Sue, where are you?' I wanted to answer – to say – 'Here I am!' and jump up on him, as I did when I was a little girl, inhale his tobacco, tweedy scent; how safe he made me feel, how special.

My father and I; c1965

This was a kind of "Hide-and-Seek" we played, my father and I. When my father returned home from work or a business trip, he would call out: *"Amy Sue, where are you?"* His glee in finding me was more than a game. His homecoming was my return to safety. Now, I hear the familiar rhyme and envision my father bouncing me in ocean waves where he is teaching me to swim. I lose sight of him now and then. Then I hear the whistle and *'Amy Sue, where are you?'*

'Here I am,' I want to say. 'But where are YOU?'

Days later, I become a fraction more awake and aware in the 'new' hospital. I have no idea where I am. When I heard the name "Valhalla," it frightened me. Valhalla is the after death "heaven" of the Norseman. Lost in a blizzard of snow, pain, drugs and machines, I could easily have believed I was in Viking Heaven or Hell – Valhalla was where the Vikings who died in battle went. The Vikings who didn't die in battle went to some awful place.

In actuality, this Valhalla, "my" Valhalla was a town in Westchester County, New York and home to the state-of-the-art critical care hospital, Westchester Medical Center, famous for its world class Burn and Trauma Center, Cancer Care facility, and innovative Heart Care facilities. I could not have been in a more expert place to deal with my myriad of conflicting crises.

Night became day and day became night. Eyes still swollen shut, I heard strange voices telling my husband and siblings my actual condition; very grave, touch and go. My critical-stage lymphoma needed treatment and, with the complications of Lupus, I had to begin at once. I never welcomed drugged sleep more as I tried to reach out to the dissolving voice of my father saying: *'Amy... Sue...where... are... you?'* Only when I was unconscious did I feel no pain.

Does the dying person see their life flash before their eyes? Maybe. My life played like a home movie on the back of my sealed lids. Perhaps as self-therapy, I reviewed the "Happy Times" before the chaotic, destructive era that seized our home, broke it and perhaps me, in two. It is only now, coming through death into life again, that I can consider how much my childhood affected my health. To look back, is to seek the answer to the riddle of my bizarre conjoined illnesses.

Tolstoy famously said in Anna Karenina —"Happy families are all alike" and "unhappy families are all unhappy in their own way." My family managed to be both. This was my first "Before" and "After" situation in the ongoing dichotomy of my life. In the sunny "Before,"there was a happy, albeit unconventional family.

Children accept the world they enter, as they know no other. I "awoke" to life in a large family of two parents and four brothers and sisters – two of each sex, with an unusual age span and history. The mood of our home was cheery even if I sensed early on, that my "place" in the family was singular: I was the only child my parents had

24

had together. The other children were offspring of their separate earlier marriages. My father had a son and daughter and so did my mother. They had left a history of divorce and entered the initially sunny fields of a "new start," new marriage, and new baby.

I was the new baby. I was their baby.

To say I was the youngest in a blended family is an understatement. I had two older brothers, Stephen and Howard, and two older sisters – both named Carla. When I was a little girl, I didn't understand why. There was always the family project at school and I drew my sisters dubbed "Little Carla" and "Big Carla." Then, from both classmates and teachers, the "whys" would start: Why do you have two sisters named Carla? My responses: "I don't know." Or, "My parents liked the name?" And that's when I became a keen observer at home. I had to figure out what the hell was going on. Why DID I have two sisters named Carla?

CONDENSED FAMILY TREE

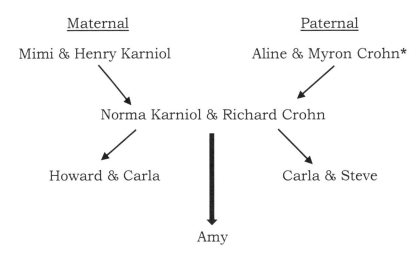

<u>Maternal</u>   <u>Paternal</u>

Mimi & Henry Karniol   Aline & Myron Crohn*

Norma Karniol & Richard Crohn

Howard & Carla   Carla & Steve

Amy

Brother of Burrill B. Crohn, M.D., physician who discovered Crohn's Disease

25

Upon my birth, my father's two children from his first marriage were already older teens: "Big Carla" was 18 and away at college; Stephen was 14 and splitting his time between his mother's home and ours. My mother's two children from her first marriage were Howard, age nine (who wrote a loving note to her when I was born adding: "P.S. Did it have to be a girl?") and "Little Carla," age four. However, there was a clear divide: My mother's daughter and son, my father's daughter and son, and me – the only child of their union.

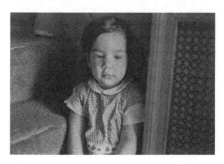

Me at about one year.

As the youngest in this strange family, I became adept at surveillance. I was the hidden, silent observer, recording memories and understandings that sometimes made sense but most often, didn't. I learned to listen really well, even when my parents spoke in French, German, Yiddish, or – in my mother's case – Hungarian, a guttural, sing-song language that revealed her Gypsy heritage.

They were so different from one another – my father and mother – yet they were so alike in that both were total iconoclasts and eccentrics; and each was connected to more famous relatives. For a while, the chemistry worked and I remember a time when I had a mother and father who loved one another and the mood in the house was an updraft of good spirits; there were wonderful meals cooked by my mother and my father played fanciful games with me and showed me the fabulous secrets of his photographic darkroom.

Oh, the darkroom. It was also my father's combination den and office and I was the only one who wanted and was allowed to stay in there with him for hours, fiddling with the cigar bands that he kept in a cigar box, playing "office," or stringing together paper clips. His newly-developed photographs with that deliciously chemical smell hung from a line with clothespins. I would watch with keen interest as he would turn out the lights leaving only the allowed amber safelight on. Then he used special wooden tongs to swirl the blank photo paper in dank and sharp smelling chemical tubs. Black and white images would appear and I was enthralled, especially when they were pictures of me. I viewed them as his portraits of love for me. I basked in the black light. Oh how I loved him and thought he loved me. Then.

Those were the periods in the early years of my childhood when Mom was joyful and Dad/Step-Dad was home. Friends visited. Full meals were cooked and served. The arts and crafts table was busy. I remember the peals of laughter when I found out that our dinner, tongue, was actually a cow's tongue. My father's laughter was especially infectious.

During the happy times at home, our nicknames were used. I was called Prune by my parents because I loved staying in the bath for so long, and the skin on my fingertips would wrinkle. I was also Boodrey and Pudding and Amila, the 'uh–la' a common ending to names when those of Jewish descent speak fondly of someone. Other times I was Pruneville or Boodreyville, all alternate terms of endearment. Little Carla was Tutu or Tutuloo. My parents called each other "Iggle." Only Howard bore the hump of inglorious nicknames my father created, a puzzle I could not solve. If there were endearing nicknames for Howard in our happy household, they existed between my mother and Howard alone.

Then there was "The Basement." This was a real basement, not finished. The basement had a dirt floor and it was cold and damp. We had a storage freezer down there and, only during rare moments of bravery, would Little Carla and I venture down to its depths on rickety stairs. There were lots of boxes and a huge rectangular, top loading freezer. If my mother asked me to go get something from the freezer, I wouldn't do it, afraid that somehow I would fall and get trapped inside and she wouldn't look for me.

At other times, bikes and sleds were hauled out and we kids would go off into the neighborhood for the entire day, stopping home only to eat or drink or to use the bathroom. All the neighborhood children loved my mother's hot chocolate and she would mix it up from original Hershey's® Cocoa and real milk and serve it with good cheer. We played traditional sidewalk games such as Hopscotch and Jacks and running games, Tag, Spud and Hide-and-Seek. One of my first friends recalls how, on a rainy day with nothing to do, my mother suggested that we set up a store using all her household goods and more. We played "store" for hours and my mother was our single optimistic shopper. That day, I basked with pride in her.

I actually did get "lost" once, not that I knew it. With Little Carla, I had wandered about a block away to visit friends when all of a sudden my mother and father burst in to the neighbor's house. They cried out: "Ahhh! There she is!" At the ripe age of about three, I burst into tears. I didn't know I was lost, but kisses and hugs from both my parents ensued, a rare treat for us to enjoy as a trio.

Because of my father's constant business trips, I didn't often see my parents together and it was even more rare an occasion to see them enjoying each other's company. One rather innocuous memory is of a fairly benign argument I had with my parents in the kitchen. There were newspapers on the floor because my mother had just mopped. I am stomping my feet and demanding to know why I do not have to go to school on my birthday. My mother and father are laughing and jointly enjoying the repartee. "Why?" I ask. "Everyone has to go to school on their birthday."

"But you don't," my mother said with a smirk. I looked beseechingly at my Dad and he said with a sly smile: "Nope, you don't," and together they laughed out loud. Finally, one of them gave me the answer. My birthday, August 26th, is in the summer. "Oh," I said meekly, proven wrong. More laughter by all three of us followed.

For many years, in our odd little home, there was an aura of wealth and sophistication without any sustaining evidence. We were all well-read and cultured, traveled back and forth to New York City to visit museums, go to plays, and see our wealthy, erudite cousins. Conversation amongst us was very adult. We had 'going out' clothes and often ate at restaurants. One glaring omission was religion. We did not speak of it; nor acknowledge or celebrate our Jewish roots. We celebrated Christmas and Easter because they were fun; I never knew their religious significance. We were taught to choose our own religion and that, in of itself, remained a puzzle to me until I was a wife and mother.

Always, there was this quality of culture, which harkened back to privilege and cultivated backgrounds that each of my parents had – my father's medical royalty and my mother's Hungarian "intelligentsia." Her grandfather had been a famous Hungarian cantor with a world class voice.

We lived in a world of fine music and cultural outings. There were Carnegie Hall concerts (box seats) during which I would invariably fall asleep with the classical orchestra alternately lulling or boring me. I can still remember how I climbed up and through the velvet ropes and heard the orchestra tune up, a gleeful sound. In this arena, both my mother and my brother Howard's knowledge would surpass my father's and I was secretly pleased to know that Howard was good at something that my father was not. Later, Howard mastered several instruments and worked as both a seasoned musician and in media production, gigs he still enjoys today.

There were weekend vacations at the Rye Town Hilton (they had a pool) and summers in the Catskills or Rhode Island. For a week to three weeks, my mother would set up house in the little summer cabins we occupied. My father would relax; smoke his pipe, read a book. Little Carla and I would make friends with the local or other visiting children and run, unfettered, all day long. We'd swim in pools, play outdoor games that we learned from new friends, and explore marshes, creeks, and the hidden, wooded areas and – best of all in Rhode Island – the beach and ocean.

The first "shadow" to our sunny start as a family was my father's intense dislike of Howard. By choice, Howard never joined us on our vacations. My brother, Howard was the enigma – and perhaps he was "the canary in the cave" foretelling danger in the family. Nine years older than me, he was beyond my reach both physically and emotionally. He had lots of friends, which made me jealous at times, and he was seldom home. His room, next to Little Carla's and mine, was filled with boy things that scared me – a huge Dr. Spock poster, a life-like gorilla bank, and action comic books.

He had discovered music as his refuge from home, being handed the French horn because it was the only instrument nobody else in the high school orchestra chose. A particularly vivid memory is seeing his tongue blood red and black and blue after a dentist accidentally drilled through it. This catastrophe had my mother in tears thinking his horn-playing career was over; but it healed and he continued to play.

On Howard's brief "visits" home, he was always kind to me and his big smile made me feel warm and loved. After teasing or tickling me, he would retreat to his sanctuary – his bedroom and close the door. Often, I would hear classical music playing softly from his record player.

My father would not allow Howard to practice his French horn in the house because it was too loud. Howard would grab a chair, his horn, sheet music and stand and venture down the block to a very large, isolated grassy park. He would choose a spot in the middle of the tall grass, far away from the small cement playground. He would play and play until a neighbor complained or he was finished. Enamored, I accompanied him at least once, sitting enraptured in the tall grass. He was so talented and my heart ached for him as, at home, the only attention he received from my father was negative. I never could understand why. More worrisome to me was Howard's relationship with Little Carla, his biological sister. There was no explanation for Howard's obvious dislike for his sister, but it was palpable.

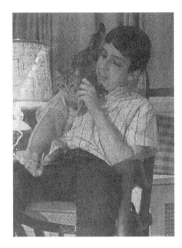

My brother, Howard, and one of our many cats.

As a young woman, I believe I figured out the dynamic. Upon Little Carla's birth, Howard was nearly five and madly in love with his own father. Timing is everything and that is when his father was diagnosed with severe mental illness and had to leave home to be properly treated – for good. I can only surmise that the event of his sister's birth coinciding with his father's departure left him with an absence of feeling towards her through no fault of her own. Speaking with Howard today, however, he talks more of his extreme love for our mother and her mother, Mimi (who adored him and little Carla but had no use for me, and dismissed me as "little whatsername") and how he treasured his alone time with both of them as a young boy. Then, it seems his father's departure, sister's arrival and, soon after, the creation of a blended family with my father and me and two step-siblings left Howard bereft and adrift.

While she was a source of pain for my brother, Little Carla (or Tutu) was close to me, in every sense. In our shared bedroom, Tutu and I were co-conspirators in laughter and light but harsh enemies when we fought. Four years older, Tutu was my big sister. She was tall. I was short. She had shoulder-length, curly light brown hair. I had dark brown, straight hair and her light blue eyes certainly didn't match my deep brown. We didn't resemble each other at all and we couldn't share clothes, even though we tried.

Her personality was somewhat serious and self-effacing but when she'd laugh (and I'd do anything to make her laugh), it was like a joyful song and infectious. We spent a lot of time together avoiding our mother, and we had our "inside" jokes just like other siblings. One that endures is calling each other "Pustefix," a brand of soap bubbles in plastic bear bottles that we received as a gift one Christmas. We thought the German name was very funny. In our funky house, Little Carla's kindness and devotion to me was unmatched. When we fought over sharing toys or other indiscriminate stuff, we'd quickly recover.

As youngsters, we were jointly ecstatic when the Avon Lady knocked and we could comb through the makeup items with our mother; we were allowed to try on cosmetics ourselves. Mom would then give us her discarded makeup and that was messy fun. We had secret games and codes and we made up stories. We had a shared friend, Antoinette,* and the three of us were creative in our game-playing and planned family performances. From a loud Italian family with many older brothers, Antoinette brought a hint of danger. She could make Little Carla and me do almost anything she said including making out with our bedposts pretending they were John, Paul, George and Ringo.

Little Carla taught me board games and Pig Latin and helped me with my homework. She read me books and, on Friday nights, we would watch The Brady Bunch and The Partridge Family in our bedroom. Little Carla was awkward at school and subject to teasing and bullying. With schoolmates, she remained soft while I grew tough, and a few times, I remember going out to find her tormentors to punish them by yelling and raising my little fists. I was barely five feet tall.

At home, though, Little Carla was my hero. Four years older, she was worldly. I watched her for cues on how to behave around our mother. Little Carla knew how to "dance" around our mother and she would please her by performing on demand; either singing (Little Carla inherited a beautiful voice) or acting a scene from a play she was in at the time (I recall Ophelia in Hamlet but there were others). I also knew exactly how to get a rise out of Little Carla when I wanted to be mean.

Because of "Little Carla," also known as Tutu, I was able to remain the imp while she protected me in the home.

Little Carla would rub my back at night to help me fall asleep, something I still enjoy if I can cajole my husband into giving me long backrubs. When the fighting between my Mom and Dad became too loud, we would retreat to our room as a hideout. It was then that my mother started pulling Little Carla away and inappropriately confiding issues with my father to her as she would to a peer.

Secretly, I was glad that Little Carla was my mother's daughter and I was my Dad's. My mother scared me too much and it enabled me to slip easily from her grasp. Little Carla was not so lucky and still grapples with the conspiracy against my father and his children that my mother foisted upon her prior to and during our parents' separation and divorce.

With one half-sister, Big Carla, 18 years older, a half-brother, Steve, 14 years older, a brother, Howard, nine years older, and another sister, Little Carla, four years older, I was the last and the least it seemed; the little girl lost among the siblings and the marital wars. I also had a sense, from the very beginning of my life, that my mother favored her Tutu. While my youngest half-sister, just four years older than me, was my best friend she was also my enemy; true to form for the closest siblings.

Left to right: Steve, "Little Carla," me, "Big Carla," and Howard in our backyard in Mamaroneck, New York in 1961

Sometimes, my mother would exclude me and "invite" Tutu "in." During lazy Saturdays at home, Tutu was summoned onto my mother's bed and played numerous games and enjoyed countless snacks there. I was not invited but in the middle of the night, I was allowed to crawl in and take comfort from the warmth of my mother's body. This maternal animal instinct was some comfort but I knew I was not her favorite, that I was somehow not adored but only tolerated. Later, matters would go far below this low standard.

At the time my father made up for my mother's attitude with his delight in me, his baby girl. I adored my handsome father from the start. Even though, then, in the beginning, my mother was not the disturbed woman she later became; I was always "Daddy's Girl." Who could resist my father? Not many. He was fun; he would sweep me up in his arms, play a thousand games, "loved me to death," as they say. I was going to be the baby daughter he really raised – Big Carla, born when my father was a medic during World War II, was already grown and away.

The Camel and the Spider

Daddy had great stories and he could and would succeed – with the same wild abandon that I later discovered he often failed at what he did. Always struggling and ever proud, he entertained me with tales of how he started his career after the war as a sales rep for Penguin Books. He had to transport a live penguin along his sales route, keeping the arctic bird in hotel room bathtubs. P.T. Barnum started a great public relations trick parading animals around for publicity for his circus and my Dad was proud to be that kind of huckster. He came by it naturally. During The Depression his mother, brother and he were often moving out of apartments in the middle of the night to avoid a rent payment and his oft-missing father was the black sheep of the illustrious Crohn clan.

My Dad, the polished salesman.

My Daddy was a World War II vet and, of course, a conscientious objector yet! He was a medic who refused to carry a gun. His stories would mesmerize me. *The-hell-with-not-carrying-guns* moment came when he and his unit very quickly learned that the Red Cross on top of their medical tent was the enemy's target! After covering the Red Cross with tarp he led his men from France into a German storage shack and stole all their weapons. There they were: A bunch of young, newly trained medics packing with my Dad as the ringleader. Hysterical.

Sergeant Dad leading the march.

To this day, his snippet of a verboten war diary mesmerizes me Entitled "Memoirs" – *An Abridgement of the travels of the 115ᵗʰ Medical Battalion Clearing Company in combat from 7 September 1944 to VE Day, the 8ᵗʰ of May 1945* is included as an appendix. His soldiers knew his as a young man as I knew him as older: stubborn, loyal, full of bullshit yet true. I came across a poem in his old army papers written by a G.I. buddy. Whenever I read it, I smile.

There's a guy in the Army,
Named Sergeant O'Crohn,
Who keeps a guy working
Like a G.D. old drone.

He starts in the morning
With that dreary old tune,
"Come on and snap to it
We'll finish this soon.

He sweats and he hollers
And pours it on thick
But you know in your heart
He's a champion "Brick."

There are bricks made of silver
And bricks made of gold
And he's one of the latter,
No need to be told.

He's such a damn faker
My heart fills with shame
That a guy of his type,
Has an "O" in his name.

-     "Garrigan"

    Fast talker, natural con man (for surely he believed in some of his promotions) – my Daddy was an anomaly, all smoke and mirrors but also a great innovator in creating first-of-their-kind direct mail fund raising campaigns for not-for-profit agencies like Save the Children, Care, Project Hope, and a true believer in utopia; or the kind of socialism that would provide for everyone throughout his or her lifetime.

    He was proud to say he was Blacklisted during the McCarthy era (never knew if that was true or not) and that his middle name was Jehosephat (It wasn't. It was Julius). This was the lifelong issue with my father – what was true, what was a fib, and what was a dangerous damaging deception? The charm was so abundant. He also believed he was reincarnated from a camel or at least he liked to say he was. He collected camel figurines – camels, loping along the desert, camels at rest, camels eating, camels carrying Arabs… I have kept some of his collection but hide it because if people see them, they give me more camels. And I don't believe I was reincarnated from a camel.

What appealed to my father about these ungainly lumpy animals? That they lived, as he did, off the "hump," in his case, an advance of cash? That they always managed to cross the desert? That they could survive where and when other living creatures failed? After his death, I found this ode to camels among his papers and it aptly describes why camels and his personality meshed:

I WANT TO BE A CAMEL

By: Stella Fisher Burgess[1]

"I want to be an angel," was once the lyric cry.
Then let such go be angels, Heaven speed them! – But not I!
I want to be a camel and with the camels stand,
With no career, no destiny, no strategic work at hand.

"For angels must on missions go, and have at mercy's beck,
And social service is their forte and flying round like heck;
But camels feel no mighty urge, nor duty's pushing palm,
They never do committee work, not rush to prayer or psalm.

"I want to be a camel and like a camel grace
With majesty and dignity my individual pace;
Oblivious to schedules and to projects I would be
And wholly deaf to crises and to opportunity.

"As to raiment, imperturbable; serene in winter's fur
And calm in spring when off it drops as if moth-eaten were.
Impervious to climate, be it Peking dust or mud;
Ye gods! grant me a camel's life and time to chew my cud!"

---

[1] Author of A Peking Caravan (1920) and Toward the Summit (1948)

My Dad with one of his favorite camel statues; c1982.

One of my earliest memories is of being in the backyard of our small rental house in Mamaroneck, New York, in my footy pajamas with my Mom and Dad (he, with camera). She snatched away my favorite teddy bear to make me cry while my Dad snapped photos. The picture was a phony – it was for one of his ad campaigns. In 1963, I was one of the "poor starving children" pictured on Dad's direct mail appeals for CARE. I never did find out who the other kid was. Years later, in a bed in the ICU, it crossed my mind that there may have been some emotional truth in that photograph. At the time the picture was snapped? I wanted the teddy bear! And I thought Daddy was the hero for "rescuing" the bear – and me.

Me, on left, holding a small tin pot.

My father received accolades upon accolades from the many, many worthy organizations and their patrons whom he helped subsidize through his hard work, including President Jimmy Carter's campaign. I recently donated his papers and correspondence with President Carter and his aides to the Jimmy Carter Library and Museum in Atlanta, Georgia. As great as his talent for raising money for others was, he couldn't consistently meet the financial or emotional needs of his own family.

Dick, as he was known by his colleagues and friends, got by on charm and flim flam – and over the years, this veneer wore thin and I came to see the "underside" of a man who may have inherited his "black sheep" genes from the lone irresponsible Crohn of a major family legacy. Gradually, the façade was exposed and I began to realize much of what he said was false or suspect. After all, his middle name was not Jehosephat. It was Julius. If he could lie about his name, what did he ever say that was true?

Dad, in full charm, at a business event.

Was his entire "good cause" promotional career a scam? Even now, I don't think so. My father had a true passion for aiding the underprivileged and believing in some sort of American utopia, even though he could barely keep food on our table. Perhaps he was an irony – partly real and partly fake.

The one solid truth about my father was…he was a Crohn.

Very early in my childhood, I became aware that I belonged to a famous, wealthy family but that the fame and wealth did not extend to our little branch. The history is this: My great uncle, prominent physician Dr. Burrill Crohn, was one of 13 children born to Leah and Burrill Crohn, Sr. Each of the 12 who survived childhood became a wealthy professional, a doctor, teacher, or lawyer and lived in Upper East Side Manhattan splendor – all except my grandpa, Myron ("Mike"), the proverbial "Black Sheep," a "na'er do well" who must have contributed the flim -flam gene to my father.

My Great Uncle Burrill B. Crohn, M.D. (1884-1983)

My father was the nephew of the celebrated Dr. Burrill Crohn who discovered the terrible intestinal disease, Crohn's disease. This celebrity connection had its odd perks. There were birthday parties for Uncle Burrill at fancy hotels where we danced the Hupsy Klupsey, the Crohn's marriage initiation dance. Who was this famous man? Why, every five years, did my family go to a first class, five star New York City hotel to celebrate his birthday in a huge Crohn reunion? The celebrations were exhilarating and creepy at the same time. Beneath all the dancing, tinkle of glasses, high-style gourmet food, there lingered a disease. And the specter of Crohn's disease sufferers, emaciated and knotted in agony, waited, unasked to dance, on the sidelines.

All the Crohn men looked like bull dogs. The "Hupsy Klupsey," was as awkward as it sounded – an erratic fox trot. The last party I attended, I was 15 years old. I spent the evening with another teen Crohn girl examining our reflections in the ladies room mirror. ("Twins," we exclaimed.) But why wasn't my somewhat-nuclear family included throughout the year in the "regular family" celebrations?

The answer came easily since it was most probably because my grandfather Mike was the scandal of this prosperous, accomplished family. Grandpa Mike, I never met ya but your stories are legend: The gambler, drinker, womanizer, who always mooched off his family, always left his wives and girlfriends but – you betcha – the life of the party, always. So the relatives would shake their heads and frown a bit when my lineage was revealed at these reunions. Oh, you're Mike's granddaughter. Hmmm. Tsk tsk. Chuckle, chuckle. My Dad, Richard J. Crohn, didn't seem to mind. In fact, he was proud to be the rebel and I suppose all the years he had to wear his name on his jacket lapel steeled him to the whispered stories and nods of disapproval.

From what I understand, for many years during The Depression, my father withstood his relative poverty, as care packages would arrive with fair regularity from the rich relatives – a bounty that he, his brother and his mother could not turn away even when the missing Mike was nowhere to be found. He also adapted when they moved in the middle of the night (again) to avoid a month's rent and Mike couldn't find them.

My grandmother, Aline Lyon, whether she knew so or not, was slated to marry the soon-to-be-famous Dr. Burrill Crohn. A not uncommon practice among wealthy and/or culturally significant families of that era, the Crohns and the Lyons were not indifferent to match-making. Yet Aline was an independent young woman. Instead of marrying Burrill, she chose instead to marry a true love outside of the families' inner circle. This non-Crohn husband drowned at Orchard Beach before their first anniversary, uncannily after a scolding by her own father that he hoped the young husband would do just that since he was so disappointed in their union. As some sort of booby prize, Aline was then awarded Myron (Mike) Crohn as her second husband, and my Granny obeyed.

But my feisty Granny Aline loved romance, drama, marriage or all three. Post her divorce from Mike after 11 years, she was married twice more to the same man; Joe Popper – a New York City horse and buggy driver. She died while my mother was pregnant with me; thus my being named after her utilizing the "A" from her first name as is Jewish tradition. Aline ("Granny") has always been described to me as a woman of determination, intelligence and great fortitude, as evidenced by this letter written to the New York Times in 1944:

TO THE EDITOR OF THE NEW YORK TIMES

I am a hospital volunteer worker at one of the hospitals and I am hoping this letter will perhaps wake up some women who idle away their time at card games or teas when they could be doing good work.

There is a serious shortage of nurses and the clinics that care for people who cannot afford independent care at home are badly in need of help.

The volunteers do good work and many women could spare a few hours a day to help until this war is over and things return to normal. Won't women please consider this matter and try to help? It is not only a patriotic duty but an act of human kindness.

Aline Popper

New York, Nov. 15, 1944

Granny, in stories related to me by relatives who were lucky enough to know her, was a treasured soul. Big Carla recalls that she was her favorite grandmother who remained very close with Big Carla and Steve's own mother, Jan (my father's first wife) even after they divorced. Some of Granny Aline's recipes endure as well, especially her unusual, sink-to-the-bottom-of-the-bowl matzo ball soup that Big Carla still makes every Thanksgiving along with sponge cupcakes with dark chocolate icing. She was also "crazy in love," says my sister, with her sons and grandchildren.

My brother recalls being told that, as a young girl, Granny Aline didn't walk but skipped around her family's lovely brownstone on 95th Street, between Park and Lexington Avenues where she was raised. She played piano with her own mother with great skill.

My Uncle Ted, Granny, and my Dad c1943

During The Depression, barely scraping by to feed her kids, she would take my Dad and his brother, Theodore, to see all the greatest vaudeville acts. Off they went from Washington Heights to journey to The Great White Way and enjoy a full day of uplifting humor, dance and song, escaping harsher realties; excursions my father would later take our family to do the same.

Granny's love of reading inspired my Dad to immerse himself in novels. By age five, he was staying up all night with a flashlight to read books under his blankets. All his life, he read five to six books a week. One of my aunts worked for the New York City Board of Education and peeked in my Dad's school file. She learned that he had the highest IQ of any student in the entire New York City school system. I love that Granny and my Daddy enjoyed a lifelong word game in which she would toss a word out for him to define. Often, he answered correctly. To her delight, however, he missed just as often.

One story that breaks my heart is how, during the Depression, Granny arrived with her two young sons at a New York City synagogue to participate in holiday services. Granny was turned away because she couldn't afford the tickets. This is why my father told me he never again acknowledged his Jewish religion.

As a Depression-era mother with a wayward husband, my favorite Granny tales are those that my father told me including how at about age 12, he assumed the role of man-of-the-house by taking every odd job he could, including delivering flowers by subway. Finally, I can only imagine her maternal horror when, as a very young boy, my father's tonsils were removed while he lay on the ironing board in the living room of their flat!

The famous Crohn connection suffered a break in 1983. The birthday parties ceased upon Burrill's death at age 99. But the legacy continued – my name was a disease. Was it destiny then, that disease would seize me, distort my life? In the face of my odds, I might have been better off with my namesake disease: A Crohn with Crohn's disease.

* * *

My mother, Norma Karniol Crohn, was a mix of gray shadow and bright, colorful light – but, in the end, the shadow overwhelmed her. As in my father's family background, my mother, too, was descended from someone very famous. Her grandfather, the Cantor Alter Yehiel Karniol (1855–1929) was revered for his range which extended from bass to lyric tenor. He possessed a beautiful mezzovoce, a falsetto like a soprano, and a coloratura that ranged through four octaves.

At an early age, my great grandfather moved from Poland to Hungary where, after apprenticeship with the famous cantor, Moshe Lutzker, he occupied many important posts, notably one in Finfkirchen, which made his name famous through the country. In 1893 the Hungarian Congregation Ohab Zedek invited him to New York, where he remained five years. Unhappy because of dictatorial synagogue officials, he accepted a call to the Great Synagogue of Odessa in 1898. Disturbed by the pogroms of 1905, my great-grandpa returned to New York. Here he served the Rumanian Synagogue,

Shaarei Zedek, and finally returned to Ohab Zedek. He retired because of increasing troubles with synagogue officers.

Of him Cantor Shmuel Vigoda (1894–1990) has written: "He was a true baal tefillah, an amazing 'zoger' who poured out his heart in fervent prayer." Not easily translated for the lay person, his personal style can be described as not just someone who sings operatically in the classic cantorial style, but someone who is deeply connected to the prayers and leads from a simpler, more "everyman" place. Cantor Karniol also was an outstanding improviser. Jacob Rapaport, a recognized liturgical composer and president of the Jewish Ministers and Cantors Association, once challenged him to improvise one of Rapaport's recorded selections. To the great delight of the assembled cantors, my great-grandfather, without hesitation, created a totally new musical setting for the text.

My Great Grandfather Alter Yehiel Karniol (1855–1929).

Although idolized by his peers, he died in abject poverty. His grave remained without a headstone for eight years. While he was still alive, one of his admirers offered to pay for publication of his works. Great-Grandpa refused, however, and so only his recordings remain as a testament to his significance in 20th century cantorial art.

His echoes in her family and in her blood were palpable. I could listen to the rare recordings and his voice filled our home with an exquisite melancholy that was prophetic. My mother resembled her

46

grandfather – with his deep black bottomless gaze – and in an uncanny way, sometimes I see his profound grief reflected back in my own mirror.

If my father's side was enriched but haunted by a disease, my mother's resonated with beautiful mournfulness. Through the cyber miracle of the web, I can still listen to my great grandfather's soulful song – as if he grieved for what was ahead for us all.

Great Grandpa Karniol imbued my mother with a great love and knowledge of music, particularly classical and opera. She spoke with extreme love for her own father and especially enjoyed the time during the Depression when she and her mother moved upstate to be near her father when he was residing in a sanatorium for heart trouble. Her memories of that time and place were so vivid and lovely. She adored her father so much. As a grown woman, my mother would often keen and cry for her father.

Norma did not have the same affection for her own mother, my grandmother Mimi Karniol, who would die at age 89 in a nursing home. From birth until age 12, the only grandparent I would ever remember referred to me as "Little Whatzhername" because she never could acknowledge that my mother had divorced, remarried and had another child. I call it selective dementia. Mimi Karniol's acknowledged grandchildren were my mother's older children, Little Carla and Howard. "Little Whatzhername" which sounded very funny with a Hungarian accent, was relegated to the periphery once again.

Mimi and Henry Karniol in Budapest, Hungary c1919.

Years later, haunted by my mother's grieving love for her father while on a business trip to Saratoga, I asked my upstate New York colleagues about this place my mother described as Eden and was told it was a prison. Yet, I found that there had been, indeed, a beautiful Victorian styled sanitarium in Saratoga, New York. Established in 1913 by the MetLife Insurance Company for "its employees to regain good health," my grandpa stayed at the Mt. McGregor Sanitarium sometime in the 1930s. The Sanitarium was also used for returning war veterans as a convalescence center during the latter half of the 1940s. Afterward, New York State assumed its ownership and it had a variety of uses. In 1976, it became Mt. McGregor Correctional Facility for men, a medium security prison.

It was reassuring to discover a truth in my mother's account of her father's hospitalization for she shared another trait with my father – they were both "unreliable witnesses." They believed whatever tale they told, which made them the most dangerous and seductive breed of fantasizers; liars who may not know when they lie. My mother's first husband, she said, went "mad." Later, I had to wonder…? Perhaps it was the folie a deux? Were they both mad? What had happened that drove her out and into my father's arms? The timing is short – "Little Carla" was only a toddler or younger when she divorced her first husband and married my father. But this tale, too, proved true. The mental illness ran deep.

On 'the outside,' my mother had many friends, some who knew of her inner torments but most, did not. She also worked for many years, as a secretary in New York City, an assistant in my father's office, as a constituent liaison for a New York State Senator and then as a resource worker for different divisions of Westchester County government, including its Office for Women.

My mother taught me how to ice skate and, every winter for several years, she took me – alone – to the Ice Capades in New York City. This was a rare mother/daughter outing that gave me great joy. We would play cards together. She taught me Gold Fish, War and Gin Rummy. My mother also enlisted me in a bizarre game in which we both held lit cigarettes – she smoking both – while we burned holes in a tissue held with a rubber band over a glass. There was a dime placed in the middle of the tissue and the object was to burn holes without letting the dime fall through the holes. I was honored when she allowed me to play this very grown up game with her.

It also didn't matter to me that her raven hair, quirky choice of clothes, ever–present cigarette dangling from her lips, and interesting use of a black eyeliner pencil cast her as an imbalanced but beautiful Natalie Wood, whom she closely resembled. I also didn't mind when I saw her face in the bay window watching, waiting, and gnawing off her fingernails as I walked home from school. I thought she was just happy to see me until I heard the inevitable: "Thank God, you're home," as she clasped her hands together. It was her panic that sent lightning through me every time she said it. Her obsession with always knowing where I was finally made me nervous, too, and I ultimately, albeit subconsciously, connected her looming face in the window with that tremendous jolt of nervous charge into my body.

Her Hungarian relatives – an aunt, close cousin, husband and two children in New York City – would call and visit often, calling her Normika (Norm–ee–kah) in endearment. They, too, were eccentric and accepted my mother's bizarre behavior, perhaps ratifying it; endorsing it.

Norma, along with my father, was highly involved in the causes of the day and was particularly involved in the Civil Rights Movement. Many of our friends were African-American and there are photos of me at Baptist Church children's events and birthday parties at which I am the only white person present. It was stunning when, as a pre-teen, my African-American friends ditched me! Until then, I was truly color blind but, by the time the "Black Power" force with fists in the air took over, I no longer belonged

My parents, Richard and Norma Crohn, during good times c1963.

In my early life, I had a beautiful, playful mother who hid handmade red cardboard Valentine hearts around the house so that we children could find them with glee. She baked scrumptious gingerbread men for Christmas, squeezing all our names onto the cookies (including the extended disconnected brood) with white homemade icing. The large sweet-smelling figures sat propped on our fireplace mantle until Christmas day when we could finally eat them.

I remember walking home from school for lunch every day to find my favorite lunch – a bologna sandwich on Wonder white bread and a bowl of Campbell's chicken noodle soup on the dining table. Sometimes, my mother would even invite one of my elementary teachers home for lunch and then my mother was engaging and lovely while I sat quietly munching my sandwich and slurping my soup and she conversed with the teacher.

Mom c1968.

In the beginning years of my childhood, her cooking was delightful. We all looked forward to her dinners. I, in particular, loved her "brown meat," pot roast in a perfect blend of spices, vegetables and stew. Thanksgiving was truly a feast, all homemade and delicious. I savored the first slice of white turkey meat with crispy glazed skin that was always designated mine.

Three Housekeepers and a Cat

My mother may have cooked well (even though we all joked that her secret ingredient was ashes because the dangling cigarette from her mouth would often burn low enough to drop its ashes into the pot) but she would not clean – at all. My mother was so inept at keeping house; my father hired three successive housekeepers. Each housekeeper would arrive in the morning, put our house in order, play Mommy with us a bit, and leave after making dinner.

The first housekeeper – Caroline Potter* – was my "baby nurse." Knowing mother was incapable of taking care of me even as a lone infant; my father hired an authentic Southern black nanny. I loved her "to pieces," even when she would yell or threaten to get "the switch." She loved me too. I could tell. But "Mizzus Potter," as it turned out, had a co-dependent relationship with my mother. As long as my mother funneled as much of my Dad's money to her as possible, she'd be there to help "Mizzus Crawn," as I remember her drawl. When I was about five, she left, moving with her husband and children to another state, yet stayed in touch with "Mizzus Crawn" for many years. Then came Misty Baker.*

Me, playing and eating; c1963.

52

Much younger than 'Mizzus Potter,' Misty was a cool black chick with a big afro. She played active games with Little Carla and me, now about ages six and 10, and danced like a rock star. Little Carla and I joined in, cheerfully, wearing our Go-Go boots, mini-skirts and scarves. She brought a lot of laughter and joy into the house. When she would leave in the late afternoon, the pall would descend again and the silence would remain until my father got home which might be that night or several days later. Misty once stayed with us a whole week when my Dad took my Mom to London for a business trip. I didn't go to school and Misty didn't care. We played and laughed and it was pure pleasure.

It was during the Misty years that no one tended to my long brown hair and it was as knotted and matted as a stray dog's fur. Every now and then (usually when my Dad was scheduled to arrive home from one of his trips), my mother would hustle me into a taxi and take me to the beauty parlor where three women in the back would work furiously with combs and brushes to get the tangles out, tsk'ing and making nasty comments about my mother's lack of mothering skills while she would get her hair done in the latest sixties style. I named my first cat, Gloria, after one of these women because she never once blamed my horrible hair on me.

Later, when the marriage and the house were in ruins, there arrived the third housekeeper...but I am getting ahead of myself; for many years the system of mother being playful and cooking, being Dad's lover and friend as well as his wife, kept us going as a "semi-happy" household, but the shadows, like the dust bunnies, were accumulating in the corners.

The bright lights grew fewer and farther between as the fogginess increased and the lights dimmed more often. Thus, as a very young child, I began to rely on instinct and knew that avoiding my mother was necessary for my very well-being. I knew if I followed her lead, I would dissolve into hysterics, something I sensed my beloved Tutu could do.

Me, playing gypsy; c1967. I 'read' the neighborhood kids' fortunes in the double swing in the background. I charged them 10 cents

With me, my mother's main emotion was to transfer her fears of disease into her youngest daughter. My mother herself claimed numerous vague illnesses and left serious instructions to have "I Told You I Was Sick" engraved on her tombstone.

"I Told You I Was Sick" might as well have been a post script on my forehead. My mother most likely suffered from what would be diagnosed today as Munchausen's Syndrome by Proxy, an unheard of phenomenon in the suburban sixties. Thus, my irrational fears about illness were fostered early as she began each day with "you don't look like you're feeling well" and took me from doctor to doctor exploring ailments that supposedly afflicted me. Later, I swung the opposite way and was too flippant about symptoms and signals of illness, attributing them all to my mother's years-long anxiety.

Very early in my life, my mother began to vacillate between hiding in the shadows in her bedroom for days on end, or craving the spotlight. She extended that desire for the bright light of fame to shine upon her children. My mother's absolute, star-struck mania almost convinced Howard, Little Carla and me along with my father's son,

54

Steve, that we were destined for greatness as – in age order – an artist, musician, actress and writer. With great determination, we fulfilled these stage roles she had created and pursued our anointed careers with her words of, "You're going to be a star," etched in our minds. Much later, watching the character Norma Desmond, in Sunset Boulevard, I realized how mad my mother really was. Gloria Swanson and Bette Davis were my mother's favorite actresses. Their movies still terrify me and evoke my mother in her rapid decline.

We drew, painted, sang, played instruments (by the time I was 14-years-old, I had taken lessons in recorder, flute, drums, piano, and guitar), performed, wrote plays and books and gave it all to Mom who would be gleeful for brief moments, reveling in our "star" accomplishments. While the four of us had some minor successes in our respective areas of creative strength, none of us has ever made much more than a decent living pursuing our individual arts. We resorted to practical jobs and careers to put food on our own tables.

In an odd lot family such as mine, it was only "natural" perhaps that some siblings would fare a bit better than others while we played out our roles in what turned out to be a short run show– the Norma/Richard marriage. But when did it all start to come apart? When did the shadow stop being intermittent and engulf our lives?

***

As I fought off the ultimate shadow in the Intensive Care Unit, I must have known it was important to find out…Something had weakened me, caused every defense in my body to collapse. What had gone wrong within me? Why was my body trying to kill itself?

As I drifted between life and death, light and dark, my memories entered the Unhappy Years…Gone was the light and laughter of my early childhood. Most often my half-siblings and I were left at home with my mother who now spent most of her time in the dark bedroom.

My father left my mother with delivery accounts from the grocery and drug stores, enough for her but barely enough for us during these especially hard times when Dad would travel all over the world doing his good works. An accomplished writer, photographer, teacher and all around handsome, charming schmoozer, my Dad had the goods to impress – others – while we at home wondered why were we last on his list?

Most alarming was how, when Dad was away, my mother's effort at maintaining a positive mood, affect and abilities left with him. His absences were predictable and I feared his leaving as much as I feared my mother staying. During those times, my mother's entire being would sag. Her shoulders would slump; she would become silent, and – more often than not – take to her room and shut the door. Sometimes I would hear her quiet but endless crying.

The third housekeeper-surrogate Mom was Jenny Wilmington* and she fit the extreme mood of the home. Black, proud with a husband and a lover, Jenny was what you would call 'a tough broad.' Every day, she watched all her "stories," as she called the soap operas, and she would whoop and holler at the television while she was ironing. "You go on, girl," she'd say every time characters would kiss. Jenny introduced me to "dirty," confession magazines and alcohol.

By now I was at least 12 and my mother had retreated completely to her bedroom, Howard moved into the city, and Little Carla was finding solace at neighbors' and friends' homes every day. I met Jenny's lover, Randall. He would visit her at our house. When Jenny wanted to be alone with Randall, she would give me a couple of sex-filled magazines like "True Confessions" that I couldn't resist reading even though I tried and, when she stayed overnight if my mother and Tutu had traveled into New York City to visit the cousins, she would buy me and my friends a bottle of Tango and/or wine and send us downstairs "to play."

* * *

As I drifted between life and death, happy memories and sad, I became aware that I was in a hospital, hooked up to machines. If I moved a limb, I heard the jangle of tubes. If I tried to speak, no sound emerged. I was vaguely aware of my lungs filling and emptying in tune with a machine behind my head that was plugged into the hole in the center of my throat. My lower legs were being compressed and released by warm encasements. I thought it was my orange tabby, Krissy, lying in bed with me, right between my legs as usual.

How the mind can play tricks. How interesting that I would conjure a cat in my ICU bed. Was this my defense mechanism – imagining one cat present and summoning the spirits of past cats that I had loved? Cats had always been an important part of my life and my comfort. And now, they surfaced – in my altered state – as a series of beloved "ghost" cats: Gloria, the sweet Calico whom I plucked from a shelter when she was a kitten and I was a five-year-old. She was my first and perhaps the most beloved of all – for she was nothing but life-affirming – she produced four litters of kittens and lived to be 18.

Cuddling one of our first cats, Marcia, c1963.

I still mourn Gloria as if a sibling passed. She slept with me all those years; I held her and regarded her sweet face in the night. When her birthing pains started, she sought me out to sit with her, not allowing anyone else in the room as she labored and delivered her many kittens, presented to me, in their little birth sacks, like gifts.

One by one, into my hospital bed, came those warm, purring cats. Next up was Marcia. A more ominous visit – as I knew, somewhere down deep, that Marcia's end was not so happy. Her skeleton was found in the bushes on our property. Cats will hide when they are dying and, in the full bloom of spring and summer, we couldn't see her in our very own hedges. At last Zelda visited, a cat my father gave to my mother when she was pregnant with me. An odd cat, Zelda bit and hissed at everyone except my mother. Zelda died of old age in my mother's bathtub. Percy, a large male gray cat also entered our life. He would disappear and reappear months later, gnawed and drawn, curling up on our fireplace hearth to heal. I always envisioned him wearing a poncho with a guitar slung over his back as he went on his travels. He was a happy guy and, finally, he left for good.

All the lost cats of my childhood revisited – one-eyed Floyd who I rescued from a horse stable, Cinnamon, one of Gloria's kittens we kept. Some people count sheep – I counted cats and eventually, they were all around me, purring to hide the sound of the grim gray machines. I lay semi-conscious imagining cats instead of life support.

Sleep came again.

Leaning on Rubble

Little by little, my eyes opened and I took an uncertain peek around the ICU. Across the hall in aquarium-like windowed units, I saw patients similarly bound to machines. I saw blurs of doctors and nurses amid the constant bustle. Then, I was able to lift a hand to touch my face. What I felt was so alarming I begged to find out: 'What is it? Why?' But I was alone. I felt a hard tube down my nose and bandages holding it in place. A trifecta of tubes on my chest snaked through my veins. Another trio of tubes was on my thigh, catheter even lower; and the horrific monster of a pipe straight through an unnatural opening in my neck, going up and down with the rhythmic whoosh of the machine behind me.

Doctors, nurses, and aides came and went with regularity, with a painful poke or prick here, an uncomfortable adjustment there or a murmured conversation among themselves as if I was not present. Not often enough, my husband and various siblings appeared. Sometimes I heard their voices, other times I squinted at their faces in the harsh light and recognized their loud hellos and saw their strained smiles. Then, quiet again.

I soon feared the lovely nurses when they approached me several times a day and night with The Suctioning Device. Unable to naturally cough up mucus, I would literally drown if the mucus were not removed. Suctioning was an indescribable procedure that rendered me breathless; my body in spasm, terror, and pain.

I dreamt, or so I thought. Some visions were dreams and some were actual procedures but I could not tell the difference. I had no one to ask. Especially vivid was one apparition. Heralded by a loud noise, I saw a wooden door in my room being pushed open, forcing an old credenza in front of it to move. Obviously, a door to nowhere 'Or to hell,' I thought. A monk (yes, a monk) in full hooded, brown burlap robe with rope tie poked his head into my room. He squeezed his form through the opening he created and materialized at the side of my bed.

He told me my brother had sent him and he said his monkish prayers. I just gazed as though in disbelief.

Again, I cried inwardly: 'I want my Daddy.'

At last, I began to stay conscious long enough to understand what the nurses, residents and doctors were saying. And I finally found out where I was – Westchester Medical Center in Valhalla, New York. I wrote a note now to ask: "Where is my family?" And I was told that they could visit just 10 minutes every hour. I lost track of hours and days. I knew only that it was night when the unit hushed and most of the lights went out or were dimmed.

During the bright hours, my husband visited often; Will stroked my head, touched my toes, wherever he could reach a part of me that was not covered with medical equipment. He had dark gray-blue circles under his eyes. His only request: "I want to hear your voice." But I could only 'speak' with my eyes as the respiratory tube torn through the layers of my neck and trachea kept me alive – and mute. My first small goal was – 'let me speak again; let me tell my husband and children I love them.'

In a vague way, I was aware that my work clients wouldn't know that I was gone. In brief moments of panic, I also understood that I had lost my work, my career – work that defined me as "Amy the self-starter, the go-getter, successful" for so many years, work that I loved and gave me a sense of worthiness.

Then, far worse, I panicked about Brett, the three-year-old foster child I'd mothered for just over a year. Would this crisis take him away, too? I scrawled a note to Will: "What about Brett? Lawyer?" He assured me he would check into it. I was uneasy thinking about how little Brett arrived only 13 months earlier. He needed me. What if he was taken away; returned to institutional life or a problematic mother who had lost custody?

I wondered why I didn't see either of my divorced parents. I wrote: "Where is Mom? Dad?" I was told that they knew of my

60

condition and were inquiring about me. I learned my mother stayed away being unable to drive, face any of the 'outlaws,' or leave her lair at home, a spacious apartment in Mamaroneck. I was not surprised by my mother's absence – I understood she was unstable, suffered from agoraphobia. But where was my Daddy? Daddy loved me so much; he would rush to my side. Wouldn't he?

My eldest sister, Big Carla, told me that Dad has chosen this time to take the vacation he and his third wife had planned in some foreign country or island but "he (was) checking in regularly." I knew Big Carla was angry and I felt as if I'd been kicked in my already empty tin chest. My heart – wherever it was – was further crushed and I didn't cry for Dad anymore.

Me, c1964.

I awoke once to see two doctors and a chemotherapy nurse leaning over me with an ominous looking bag of mushy, reddish-gray stuff. "Your cancer begs treatment," a tall handsome doctor said and the nurse stayed, squeezing this foreign matter into one of my chest tubes. I scrunched my eyes shut and conjured up The Statue. The Statue was my ultimate self-defense.

I didn't yet know of biofeedback or "visualization" when I first imagined The Statue during a particularly difficult time in my life. I was 18 and I had been left on my own by both parents. It was overwhelming to learn I had to fend for myself and I felt the world beneath me collapse; much as I felt now in this strange medical place. In its stead, or from its ashes, rose my imaginary alter-ego, The Statue.

Somehow, I incorporated my insecurities into The Statue. From the very beginning, The Statue reflected any damage done to me. On that first day nearly 16 years earlier, The Statue had a ragged crack that ran straight through its center and into the foundation. Shuddering awake, I thought a great deal about this image and tied it into my state of mind. This jagged, ragged crack meant 'take care – you're still standing,' it told me – 'but on a precarious wedge of stone. Go out and conquer but head home if you see me get worse,' my Statue revealed to me through telepathy.

Over and over again I would go – to school, to work and shut my eyes and conjure The Statue. Some days, pieces of it would be on the ground. Other times, limbs would be cracked off. On other days, The Statue would be in bits. Those days, I usually called in sick to work or missed class and stayed home caring for my wounded self, not actually understanding what the wounds were but relying on my Statue for guidance.

I relied on The Statue to monitor, even to predict my conditions. Upon the acute medical crisis in late 1996 and early 1997, my Statue was dust. It was too soon for me to marshal the strength or concentration needed to rebuild my Statue but even thinking of her must have helped. Gradually, bit by bit, she would rise from the ashes – and so would I.

Bribes and Ladders

As my mother and father became increasingly estranged, and my mother's psychiatrist prescribed the very latest in tranquilizing medications, the house became quiet, dark, and very, very dirty. By the time I was 12 and we had moved to our new house, my parents began living on separate floors. The house fulfilled its design – it really was a split level. Thus began the dank, dark days. My father's business trips were more frequent and my mother's bed became her cocoon of sorrow.

My Dad's trips became longer and longer and it soon became obvious he was having extra-marital affairs. He would bring home women "clients" for dinner and my mother would cluck cluck with her Hungarian relatives about this one and that one. Then – he moved out. They announced their separation together. Mom's drama needed tending that week, I guess and she did her best Desmond ever. My father did the talking. My mother sat stone-faced at the opposite end of the couch from him. Little Carla kneeled next to my mother. I sat in a chair, alone. I looked back and forth from my father to my mother. I don't recall his exact words but he spoke calmly and evenly while my

"Little Carla," my mother, me and my father during a rare family outing. Note our positions: My mother's daughter, Tutu, and, me, my father's daughter.

mother just stared at nothing with her head slightly tilted, shoulders slightly slumped, cigarette dangling from her fingertips, and lips held tight on her made up face.

Before my father could finish his careful words, I began crying, stood, and ran out of the room. Soon after, he came to me as I cried in my bed with Gloria alongside. He tried to reassure me; words that weren't patronizing but also held little hope for a frightened pubescent girl. Little Carla didn't come to me and I didn't blame her because as she grew into a teen, my father treated her like little more than an annoyance, one of the few love/hate conflicts I can also never reconcile with my Dad's nothing-but-loving attitude toward me in the early years. When I left my room later to use the bathroom, I saw my Mom celebrating with Drambuie, a liqueur that I've never seen anyone else drink. The house was very quiet.

When Dad left, however, so did the housekeeping money and our home descended into filth. We became afraid to turn on the kitchen lights at night because we were sure the army of roaches would overrun us. We always had up to four cats as pets and now, the cats used the floor and carpets as their litter boxes, and the flea infestation was remarkable. I could part my cat's fur and see all the little black buggers run around her body. The flea bites on my body were too numerous to count.

We endured like this for a year-and-a-half – my mother effectively "bribing" Little Carla with a jovial pact of shopping and movie watching and freedom since the 'evil' man was out of the house. I was left out and retreated even further into my room, my space, myself, in between visits to my father. In the sixth grade, I was out of school for 60 days, having such a fear of what I might or might not find when I would return home that I wouldn't leave. In fact, so crippling was the anxiety and nausea that I found I couldn't leave the house at all at times. I tried to sleep over at friends' houses and would, invariably end up feigning illness (or truly feeling awash with nausea) and come home.

I remember one such sleepover, fairly far away from my house, when my friend invited two of us to stay over. I rode my bike over (a good five miles away) and, after dinner, we all took to our bikes for fun. Riding and laughing we came close to my own neighborhood and my heart started racing and my head whizzing. I was near home and didn't want to go back to her house. Muttering something about not feeling well, I rode straight home, surprising my mother and Little Carla. I just shrugged and said I didn't want to stay over. My mother got on the phone and the sleepover was cancelled.

I was as afraid to leave home as I was to stay. It was home, after all, but I think I was most afraid of what I would or wouldn't find when I returned. So I stood sentry in my miserable anxiety-riddled body and mind; thinking that as long as I was there, I had some sort of control. Of course, I did not and my body, sensing this lack of control, reacted with headaches, a speeding heart, nausea, vomiting, sensitivity to light and daily confusion.

When over-stressed as a ten to 13-year-old, I would draw all the blinds in my room and keep it dark, watching a little television or reading, my cat always close. Needless to say, my grades in school suffered and so did my social life. Even my relationship with my father took a turn for the worse as I morphed from a vibrant, active little girl into a sullen, hypochondriacal teen.

Tough age, tough times at 13 years old, 1973.

He had forgotten, I guess, about how school phobic I was even as a young girl. In first grade, I remember sitting outside school with my mother on a low curb. She had tried, without success, to get me to stay inside but I, crying loudly, refused to stay. I stood and tried, through tears, to explain myself to her. But she just sat there, chin in one hand, cigarette in the other looking faraway. "Please, Mom, please," I was trying to say through my tears. "Help me. Don't just sit there. Please help me understand what is wrong with me." She didn't respond and just took my hand and walked me home, then retreated further into herself.

This little scene was repeated many times through elementary school. At times, I was completely "normal," most often when my father would come home singing: *"Amy Sue, where are you?"* I would immediately revive. *"Amy Sue, where are you?"* The words were enough to pull me out of my stupor of sadness.

My father reveled in my normalcy with nature outings, trips to the city, the zoo, and when we sat side-by-side watching football games on TV. We also ate at McDonalds or Walter's Hot Dogs or Cooks, all legendary restaurants in Mamaroneck, New York. The McDonalds franchise was one of the first "Golden Arches" to open, although the real arches have long since been removed. Walter's Hot Dogs is still there and can be Googled for its famous history, grilling technique, Pagoda-style building and celebrity customers. Cooks was an innovator, combining a children's game room with a cafeteria style dining room. Little Carla would accompany us on some of these trips. More frequently, as the household divide widened figuratively and – with the separation – literally, I would go alone with my father, treasuring my time with him but, secretly, mourning the loss of Little Carla.

In 1974 after my wanderlust father moved out and Little Carla went away to college, I was truly alone. Although it was clear that she was my mother's daughter and I was my father's, my sister and I were buds most of the time and she did act as a buffer between me and my mother; a shield and a reminder of my odd place in the family of so many origins. Just as my mother would drag herself out of bed to clean up for my father's many homecomings; she would do the same for my sister but not for me.

My brother Howard had ceased living with us about five years earlier when he and my father's arguments worsened and my mother paid for a rented room for him in the City where, for his own safety and sanity, he attended college.

When I was 14-years-old and living with my mother while the divorce was being finalized, I would stay as involved in school and with friends as I could or curled up in my dark room with my heavy anxiety blanket, my cat and TV in between visits with my father. All matters big and small continued to deteriorate with my mother. By the tenth time I was locked out of the house late at night after some activity at school and my mother couldn't (or wouldn't) hear the doorbell or the phone ringing when I called from the neighbor's house, I became calm — rather than upset — for the moment.

For the final time, I put the ladder against the back of the house to climb in a window. I walked into my mother's bedroom, stared at her – she was in a fetal position surrounded by beer cans (Drambuie was too expensive now). She was snoring and the TV blared. With anger, I switched off the TV which roused her and she spewed curses at me for doing so. With my heart pounding more wildly than I could ever recall, I walked into my room and spent the night plotting my escape.

Intensive Repair

A few days after being admitted to ICU, the appropriate specialists attempted to remove the respirator to see if I could breathe on my own. It was a difficult experiment as they removed the hose and tried different stoma sizes. The first was too small. They knew this because my eyes opened wide with terror when I couldn't breathe. The second one fit and it gave me a sense of reaching a first milestone. My hopes were confirmed that evening when my husband arrived and I put my finger over the hole. I was able to croak out: "Hi Will."

My husband dropped to his knees with audible sobs and then ran out of the room. Tears rolled out of my eyes with abandon – I had crossed the first of many thresholds of hope. It hurt to cry but, damn, it was better than absolute terror with no outlet at all. If time could stand still, there would be longer periods of unconsciousness, free of pain. Rarely, if ever, could I find comfort in the intensive care setting. Very rarely did I long to be conscious. The unconscious state was preferable.

Soon enough, the feeding tube team extracted the metal, bendable tube from deep in my nose, throat and stomach. "Eat, eat, eat," a male nurse ordered. "The only ones who come out of this, Amy, are the ones who eat. I've got a guy down the hall as sick as you and he'll only eat salami sandwiches. I don't care what you eat, just eat."

So when they brought the hard-boiled egg, my husband helped me pick at it and I ate. When they brought the little box of Cheerios, my husband helped me pick at them and I ate. The apple sauce, yogurt, whatever; I made attempts to swallow although there was a huge catch in my throat and the dread of any impending suctioning. I tried to sit up. This was no easy task as my body moved awkwardly with pain and tubes. By the time I got into a chair, I was exhausted and had to be put back into what they call a bed in ICU, a blow-up mattress that inexplicably deflated often and left me lying on a cold metal slab at times with no one available to re–inflate.

'The morgue?' I thought in my clouded state.

The nurses all commented on my remarkable husband; how he clipped my toenails, was there ten minutes of every hour he was allowed, and was so attentive. They bemoaned spouses who abandon their critically ill loved ones out of fear or opportunity or indifference. I lit up when the wonderful nurses came to see me. I will never forget when a night ICU nurse heard my pleas to wash my hair. I had long, very curly permed hair, and I wanted it washed, a simple but complicated request. She was slow, gentle and calm as she somehow rigged a washbasin behind my head. The soap suds and warm water transported me. For a short while, I felt human.

There were numerous medical residents, too. This was a teaching hospital and I was a curiosity. I was also practice fodder and nearly fainted when one male resident, barely 23 years old, was guided by the elder professor to remove my "swan," a soft catheter with an expandable balloon tip that is used for measuring blood pressure in the pulmonary artery. One of the wonderful nurses held my hand and spoke in a soft voice as the long procedure continued. I spit with anger at the female resident who sat cross-legged on the credenza one evening as I begged for more pain medicine only to have her tell me: "They don't want you to get addicted." I screamed silently: 'Who cares?' I cried myself to sleep in pain that night.

Then, the children were scheduled to visit. 'Oh my! Would they be afraid? How should I look?' Someone brought me a blue bandanna to tie around my neck so they wouldn't see the stoma. The covers were pulled up and tucked in as high as possible, encasing me mummy-like so they couldn't see the many invasive tubes. My husband left to pick up the children and my sister and brother helped with my feeding. So concerned with my appearance and energy for my boys, I neglected to eat more than a few bites and, later, in the hushed dark without any available food, I found that I was starving.

Daniel and Brett, two wonderful reasons to live.

Too soon, it seemed, my little boys arrived. Seven-year-old Daniel found my hand. He brought me a homemade get well card. He was wary and stayed by his Daddy. On the other hand, have-no-fear Brett, scrambled right up onto the bed, laid his head on my burning chest and kissed my face wherever he could find an open space. This pattern with the boys continued throughout the coming year as I spent most of my time in one hospital or another, a revolving door of long-term care based on the critical nature of my case. Daniel was there – watching, observing, fearful yet loving, bringing me numerous gifts and writing me special prayers and songs. Brett was in and around and on top, happy just to see me even if all he could see were my eyes.

Finally, I was moved to a regular room at Westchester Medical Center. Helped into a "real" bed, I was war torn and relieved. It was me, my bed, my telephone, my television, and my commode. 'What a relief!' I instantly fell into the best sleep in many, many months. The next days and nights were a whir: Another chemo infusion and subsequent delirium, mouth sores, hair loss ('Wow. That hurts!'); and the first bone marrow biopsy, a harrowing experience on its own.

Doctor visits were numerous including those specializing in rheumatology, neurology, pulmonology, cardiology, gastroenterology, otolaryngology, hematology, orthopedics, infectious diseases, physical therapy, and surgery. I got to know day nurses, night nurses and the simple, curious ones who wandered into my off-limits room at the far end of the hall (No more monks, thankfully).

My first brush with chemo wipeout required transfusions of both blood and platelets. There was nothing worse than hearing your oncologist say: "There is nothing else I can do" and praying for the miracle that someone else's blood products will help rejuvenate your own. Receiving the transfusions called up many more fears. 'Could the blood be tainted with AIDS? Just whose blood was this anyway? Are they using the right type? Why is it that color?' I recall mumbling in question several times: "Is it Type A positive?" I never quite heard the answer.

I was so immune compromised, my young children carrying germs weren't allowed inside. About two weeks of this quarantine ensued. Isolated, I pasted "Hello" signs to my boys on the windows so they could come to the parking lot and wave to me and I could glimpse them.

Sore, weakened, and confused, my mind often drifted. Again, I was a child – remembering, yearning, and contorted, trying to fashion some sort of reasoning about why I traveled to this hell. Earlier memories returned to me; when I was a younger girl I often would be immobilized in bed or on the sofa with one unexplained illness after another. Illness was one surefire way to get attention in my house.

When I was sick (and it was usually when my father was far away and I felt sheer panic), my mother would instantly call Fred's, the local stationary store, and order comic books, candy and toys. These would be delivered to the door and I would be occupied for the day. My mother would disappear and the day housekeeper would serve me soup, soda, crackers and ginger ale.

During some of the illnesses, my mother – who, at that time, helped out intermittently at my father's office just one block away – would go to work. She would instruct the housekeeper of the day to play Trouble® with me or keep me busy with my new Baby Alive® or other toy while I lay in her bed or mine, moving as the housekeeper cleaned each room.

One particularly awful memory is when I fell and was almost paralyzed. I was enjoying gymnastics in school so my father, in his handyman glory, rigged up a parallel bar across my doorway. Alas, he used a wooden closet bar and, swinging upside down one day, the bar broke. I fell in a heap to the floor, landing right on the nape of my neck. I was in terrible pain and spasm. My father – the medic in World War II – made sure there were no broken bones and I was, indeed, not paralyzed. Doctors were called and one visited. My parents were told to use heat to soothe the muscles that were now in spasm and I would heal up in time.

My mother ran a bubble bath for me. In my budding pre-teen state shortly before my father left for good, she did not want my father to see my naked body. My father did have a proclivity for pornographic magazines and I recall them fighting often about Playboy being left out for "everyone to see." My mother, however, did pose for sensual and naked photographs for my Dad; some of the tamer pictures were hanging in their bedroom, so I was somewhat confused by her loud protests. Sexuality was still a mystery. To me, I was still my father's child.

Once in the bath, I complained that it was too cold. In our old, rented house we often didn't have enough hot water. My mother set a tea kettle to boil while I complained and cried to my father who sat next to the tub. He was allowed in since I was covered with bubbles. In she came with the tea kettle and I whined louder. Among the bubbles, it was difficult to see where my body parts lay, but – without even trying to look – my mother stared directly into my eyes for a good second or two and poured that scalding water directly on my thigh. I screamed. My father screamed and for the next two weeks, my father tended my neck, back and a third degree burn on my leg. The scar remained visible for many years.

The sick days continued but when I would hear the familiar: *"Amy Sue, where are you?"* when my father came home for dinner or from a business trip, I would jump up laughing, and run to him. He would tickle me, do raspberries on my neck, and ask me about my day. When he learned that I had missed yet more school, a fight between my parents would ensue and, at some point, I began a round of medical tests to determine what was wrong with me.

I calmed myself with creative play. Here I brought a dead tree 'back to life' with tissue paper flowers.

I recall being tested for Meniere's disease, a disorder of the inner ear, but no test of the time revealed anything out of sync. I was fine and healthy other than fraught with anxiety. A "nervous child" the doctors said, including my beloved pediatrician, Dr. Kligler, who still made house calls. When I was in my late teens, Dr. Kligler committed suicide. At that time, so cynical with all that childhood could offer in terms of solid mentors, I said to my mother upon receiving her phone call with the news: "Well, another childhood icon shot to hell."

There were two other manifestations of my extreme childhood anxiety, both obsessive compulsive activities. The first my family nicknamed "the touchies." Before going to bed at night, I had to touch everything in my room the "right way." This touching moved beyond my room and all the way down the stairs to the living room. I remember my mother walking beside me as I did my touching ritual that could last for up to 15 minutes. She never spoke and — in my eyes and mind — I was, again, begging her, just like I did about my school phobia, to 'help me stop.' She rarely looked at me straight on, just plodded along besides me, perhaps showing her love for me in this way.

After finally going to sleep in my own bed, I would wake up when the house was dark and venture down the hall to my mother's room. Despite our emotional distance, I slept with my mother almost every night after whispering: "Mom. Can I sleep with you?" She would open the covers and I would slip in. Perhaps this was the only way I could interact with her without repercussion and snuggle next to her warmth and get to know her; her scent.

The second habit or 'tic' I suffered was licking over and above my upper lip, also ritualistically. The lip area would get very red and sore and my siblings and school mates teased me. Along with my matted hair since my mother didn't comb it and my father insisted it stay long, I wasn't cute anymore but scary, even to myself. I don't remember when either of these activities stopped but, as an adult, I still sometimes touch things "the right way."

***

After that awful evening when I entered my home via a ladder, I woke the next day packed and ready to go. After trudging two miles, I arrived at my father's apartment in a two-family house. I had a suitcase in one hand and a cat carrier, heavy with its occupant, the beloved Gloria, in the other. I knocked on his landlady's door, got the key, and let myself into his apartment. He was away on one of his business trips and I stayed in that apartment alone for two days waiting for my father to come home. The landlady checked on me, gave me food along with cat food for my precious Gloria and I felt a bit reassured knowing she lived right down the stairs. But, boy was I scared! What would my mother do? Could I stay? The phone rang over and over again. I didn't answer.

Dad returned home. He fought with my mother over custody. We went to a court-ordered psychology session and, ultimately, my mother had no choice but to permit me to stay with him because I refused to return to her. Her triumphs: 1) Revealing horrific family "secrets" including alleged sexual indiscretions committed by my father (even the raspberries on my neck), that were at worst, a last grasp at revenge and, at best, a mean–spirited attempt to make me think less of my father; and 2) Ensuring that my Dad continued to pay her my child support for the next four years even though I would be living with him.

Even as a hypochondriacal and anxious teen, I guess my Dad did still love me; 1976.

Dad and I moved to a nice town about 15 miles away and it became, in my adolescent mind, "You and me against the world," a la Helen Reddy. I started a new school and assumed the bulk of our small household's responsibilities. During my childhood with the housekeeper trio, I had learned how to roll socks, but I never learned how to do laundry, cook, or clean. Dad hired a housekeeper for a little while to help teach me. And so she did. I learned and I managed.

I did Dad's laundry and only ruined one load, staining everything pink. I did the grocery shopping and, before I turned 16, he taught me how to drive on a standard stick shift. Three short weeks after my 16th birthday, I had my driver's license. I even cooked dinners for my Dad and his clients. He still took lengthy business trips and my anxiety and heart-pounding fears would surface when I imagined life without him. If I went out with friends for the evening, when I returned home I would check to make sure Dad was breathing.

Our next door neighbor, Arlene Ogden,* a lovely young woman who was probably in her late 20s at the time, would let me sleep with her in her king-sized bed when I was scared. She was the one I went to with "female" questions and I remember Arlene helping me get ready for my senior prom. On the other side of us, in one of the very few rental apartment building complexes in Hastings, New York, lived one of the teachers in my new high school. He would also keep an eye out for me, making sure I was able to be a student as well as a housekeeper and pseudo-wife.

My illness pattern continued although I also learned, for the first time, how very needy my father was. When he was sick or had a root canal, I would get called over the loudspeaker at school to come to the office where I was instructed to go home. Unlocking our shared apartment, I would find him in distress and was required to fetch him medicines and food. When I was sick, however, he very nearly recoiled and gave me the names and telephone numbers of doctors offered by his new girlfriend. At 16, I was driving myself to a new pediatrician, gynecologist, internist, etc. and tried ever-so-hard to heal myself from my ills.

I still didn't understand that most of my illnesses were psychosomatic. The very good pediatrician I was seeing at the time did discover and point out to me that, during times of real illness, I had an elevated level of anti-nuclear antibodies (ANA) that, most probably, meant I had an auto-immune disorder. I filed that information away since she said it likely meant nothing unless I developed some more serious conditions. She didn't elaborate and I never pressed her for more information.

Then, new problems surfaced. The superintendent slipped a holiday card under our door addressed to "Mr. and Mrs. Crohn." Now 17, I felt scalded with an odd embarrassment. But my unearned discomfort soon became irrelevant. Taking after his own Dad and the Crohn clan in general, my father became a 'serial husband' and moved on to long-term relationship number three with a local woman in Hastings-on-Hudson, New York, a village known to be full of intense, extremely liberal intellectuals.

My father's new girlfriend owned her own home (splendidly large) and held a job (secure and pensioned), so when Dad sent me shakily off to Syracuse University (the only school I ever wanted to attend for its Communications Program) and told me "not to worry about money one single bit," I believed him and he gave me a credit card. Alas, it was only a matter of weeks before the Syracuse bursar's office was after us. Dad was sorry, he said, but he just did not have the money anymore. The credit cards were maxed out.

Turned out, he couldn't pay tuition at all. He had crafted a doomed business deal when he sold his own profitable company and was still up to his eyeballs paying off my mother and was going to move out of our apartment because it was too expensive. His new girlfriend could/would provide for him, once she got her divorce but – for now – he needed a small apartment to use as a mailing address so she wouldn't lose her alimony. Could I come home and help?

Already walking on Jell-O® at college, being so ill-prepared for co-ed dormitory life when I had already been living, most often, on my own for years, I panicked. After three sleepless weeks mulling over my options, I sub-consciously used the only way I knew how to get out – I got sick. In the college infirmary, tossing with sleeplessness, I muttered to myself: "Amy Sue. Where are you? Amy Sue. Where are you?" But in my haze I couldn't make sense of why I was being called to bail him out when I was the one who so desperately needed help. A refund was guaranteed only through illness. I could pay back my Dad and go home and help him.

The Lean, Mean Years

Still reeling and in a panic, I wondered just what the hell was going to be left of our home when I got there? Would he have moved out already? Where was my stuff? What was I supposed to do now? Big Carla, married with three children and living in southern New Jersey, drove all the way to Syracuse to pick me up along with my few belongings. It was a long drive and I remember we stayed overnight in a hotel. By now, I could look at my sister as a friend. She was barely 36 years old and I, a very immature18 when my Dad cut me off financially and emotionally after a tumultuously long period of being on a see-saw for the truth. Ultimately, I kept his secrets because I could be rid of him and his neediness by passing him off to his soon-to-be third wife. And, by agreeing to a bogus living arrangement, the new Mrs. Crohn-to-be (and he, by default) could keep her alimony money.

During a crisis, I'm calm and can make decisions. As a very young adult, they weren't always the wisest decisions, but without elders to guide me, I relied on survival instinct and a fierce desire to become a newspaper reporter. When I was six and in first grade all the girls in my class wanted to be nurses or teachers or Mommies. I wanted to be a writer, I said. When they laughed, I became even more determined.

In short order, I found a cheaper, one bedroom apartment in a three-family house the next town over from my Dad. His "bedroom" was the living room since he made only a pretense of living there. I enrolled in New York University and got a full-time job. I was still alone and short of cash. What can only be looked at now as serendipity, I noted a boarded up wall in the apartment. Could there be a staircase and attic overhead? I talked to the landlords to find out what was up there. The German-American, pie-on-the windowsill type of couple, could sense my excitement; the self-survival gears grinding away in my brain.

Lo' and behold, there were three finished rooms with a staircase leading down into my apartment. I asked: "Will you allow me to open up the staircase, clean the rooms and sublease?" "Sure," they said, already being protective of me and looking out for my best interests as well as their own. I posted ads for roommates and charged each of the three girls enough to cover their rent and mine. One of the "roommates" needed the place only as a ruse (as my Dad did) – she lived with her boyfriend and her parents objected. Every now and then she and her parents would show up and the rest of us would pretend we knew her. "Did you have to leave the light on all night last night, Tricia?" "Are you in on the groceries this week?"

I called my father, made an appointment to see him and we had an emotionally charged meeting at the apartment. I told him my plan and gave him no options while I stood straight and proud, arms folded across my chest, chin up – all the while envisioning my Statue. While his mouth was moving, I kept my gaze on his eyes, eyes that were questioning now: "Amy Sue, where are you?" He meant the "old" Amy, of course; the one that would yield to his edicts like putty, help him live his life rather than focus on my own. With that final meeting, I kicked Dad out for good.

Taking a good look at myself in the mirror and telling Dad to get out; 1979.

One by one, a succession of roommates came and went. I lived in the master bedroom downstairs. I went to school, worked and outwardly enjoyed my free-spirited, unencumbered life. Boyfriends, too, came and went. I had a series of "Daddies" across the country and could count on any one of them to talk to by phone or come running when I called. It was not lost on me that I sought to replace my father with an alternate, reliable man of any age. However, within the armored wall, the terror was growing and growing and growing; an abyss into which I sensed I would fall.

These were my lean, mean years. I hopped in and out of the city but started having issues with the roommates at home; one who was trying to replace me as head of household and another who let strange men in at all hours. I would have to throw out the errant roommates to keep the trust and agreement I had with my landlords. I also didn't know how to fit in – socially – with any surrogate family group. I always had a boyfriend or two but I was a misfit when it came to relationships with other women. I found solace in solitude which – while unusual – was the main reason I preferred to live alone.

After about two years, the apartment roommate drama became too much for me. But how else could I continue to go to school yet live a relatively reclusive existence without money? The brain gears started turning again and inspiration struck. Ah, become a nanny! I interviewed and landed a position with a precocious six-year-old boy with upscale parents in Scarsdale, New York. I had my own bedroom, shared a bathroom with the little guy and was able to bring my beloved Gloria, with me. Every night, I sang "How Much Is That Doggie in the Window?" over and over and over again to my charge until he fell asleep. I never really knew what his parents were doing in that precious time away from him.

I ate meals with this surrogate family, yet I was an employee. While I can't remember the little boy's name, I do remember that I liked him and his sense of humor a lot and that his parents made him eat something green at every meal – a raw pepper, celery, spinach, whatever. When they weren't home, I would give him a spoonful of mint jelly. He liked Scooby Doo and me, too.

It was a romping two months that I was able to attend NYU and be home in time for him to get off the school bus, do his homework, feed him dinner sans working parents, and get him to bed. Then, I had my solitude. Most weekends, I was free and met up with old and new friends until I was leveled yet again with an illness – this time severe mononucleosis. The pattern was becoming clearer and clearer to me, now. Stress upon stress would invariably lead to real illness.

With nowhere to go to be cared for, I tried The Mother in the two-bedroom Mamaroneck apartment she secured after the divorce was finalized, but that arrangement lasted for three days. She put me in her master bedroom with her slippery, nylon bed clothes and left me there to sweat and manage the fever with a bottle of Tylenol. My mother re-arranged herself in her apartment living room (the second bedroom was full of junk) and kept herself busy with loud television and her married boyfriend. When I would ask for something from her, the items would not be available and the girl who did grocery shopping for her wasn't coming for a few more days. When I would cry out for her in the night, her sleep was so deep from medication, she didn't hear me or, even when I tried to shake her, she did not wake.

I called my father but he hemmed and hawed as he had finally landed the great marriage gig in a Hudson River view "castle" with his new, soon-to-be wife. I called my best friend's mother and asked if I could stay with them. She said: "No. It's too contagious. I'm sorry." Stung, I called my pediatrician and she suggested I get myself to a hospital. And, so, I did. I packed my suitcase again and called a taxi. I arrived at the hospital in the dark. I noted that my Statue looked lashed with sword strikes but was still standing.

Admitted to isolation, I had "the worst case of mono they'd ever seen" and I was treated by white coated, gloved, masked nurses and doctors for about a week. My full, packed suitcase stood in the corner. This time, I was scared. This illness was real. I turned yellow, bruises popped up on my body and the word leukemia was mentioned more than once. I trusted my doctor who, after a few days, said I would, indeed, get well. It was "just mono" and to rest for a long time.

Dad visited and I kept my face towards the wall. He rambled on and on about how he was sorry and that his situation was what it was but if I wanted to come and live with him and his gal pal, I could. Not moving my face an inch, I said: "Dad, I want to come live with you." After a pause, he asked: "For how long?" The pain hit, hard. I told him to leave. I heard him shuffle and tsk, perhaps with loving hesitation, but he left. The explanation I heard later was that he and his new lover did not want adult children living with them; however, at merely 19, I pointed out that his girlfriend's daughter was barely a year-and-a-half younger than I was and she lived with them. No response. Save for two, anger-filled "summit meetings" during which we argued about money, I did not speak to my father again for 10 years.

One of the last pictures of my father and his three biological children a few years before our 10-year estrangement; 1974

Protect and Defend

Extreme fury. It's a great antidote to fear and anxiety! I was damn angry and decided then and there in that hospital bed that what happened my first 18 years was NOT going to dictate what would happen for the rest of my life. Scared? Absolutely. I resolved to grow up despite (or, in spite of) my parents; remove them as obstacles.

So, after a few phone calls, I was able to spend a comfortable and comforted three weeks with my ex-boyfriend's parents. About a year earlier, I had unceremoniously dumped Adam* and he moved on with his life, working and living with a new girlfriend. I called out to him, but he wouldn't come. His parents, however, were as close to the fictitious, loving Cleaver parents as any I ever met. Then, with some regret, I extricated myself from the nanny situation and moved down to New Jersey to live with Big Carla –family. 'Ahhh,' I thought, 'I can relax and get those gears cranking for yet another plan of action.'

It was a tense time, however, and lasted only another short two months. My dear sister was diagnosed with breast cancer. I was in charge of the house and her three children, ages nine to 13, until she and my brother-in-law returned home from Sloan Kettering in New York City. I was honored yet petrified but I had learned how to keep house well by now. I did what needed to be done with great love.

Yet I barely had had time to heal myself. These new uncertainties caused my anxiety levels to rise to new heights. Once things settled at my sister's home, I tried to get a job and an apartment near her and her family. With her help, I landed a part-time "gofer" job at a local daily newspaper ('go for' this, 'go for' that) and a small studio apartment within walking distance of my job. I think the editor hired me because, having nothing to lose, I answered the "Sex" question with "Yes" rather than a gender. He thought that was very, very clever. I figured he (at the ripe old age of approximately 45) just wanted to get in my pants but I didn't care. I wanted this job. I also started seeing my first therapist regularly on my own terms.

The job amazed me. I participated in the inner workings of a daily newspaper, even if it just meant being barked at to go out and get Kentucky Fried Chicken for everyone. But I did begin to flex my writing muscles – first with obituaries, then with photo captions and finally with news and feature articles. I was the lowest paid reporter on staff. My highest compliment was when the city desk editor, who was at most 30 years old, said I was the best caption writer he'd ever had. ('So, I do have a talent,' I thought.) Deadline was midnight and my new friends and I would go out 'til 4 a.m. I would sleep until noon. And I loved this job and its hours. In 1980, the pay was $11,000 a year and my rent was $135 a month.

But I longed to return to New York and college. I felt that I would never progress in this writing career of mine if I did not earn that college degree and, so, I resumed my plan. This long-term plan (if you could call it that at 20 years of age) was partly fueled by a happy accident. I reconnected with a friend from a few summers back when I moved in with my sister. Months before my mono diagnosis, this friend and I had planned a singles weekend in the Catskills that was still on the calendar. By the time the trip rolled around, I was recovering from *the worst-case-of-mono* and she, having gone on a blind date during the six months' time, had become engaged. There was a third girl who was going with us and on the prowl.

My friend, Deirdre,* and I made a pact: We would ski, use the spa, and never leave each other's side. As most of my clothes were still in New York, my sister lent me some of hers. We weren't looking for love or even brief lustful encounters; we just wanted a weekend vacation. Our third party thought otherwise and she unreservedly entered this bizarre weekend tableau of a Jewish singles weekend at the now-defunct Concorde Hotel while Deirdre and I stuck together like glue.

The first night there, I turned down a request for a drink and conversation from a very handsome Italian who certainly did not fit in at a Jewish singles event in the Catskills. In fact, seated at the communal table, he would occasionally whisper to his friend, a bonafide Jewish schlemiel and I was convinced that he needed an interpreter. How did he land here? From what planet?

Off we went our separate ways until Sunday morning, day of departure, when I snuck off for a solo swim in the indoor pool. And there he appeared! The handsome Italian was wearing jeans, work boots, and a red plaid wool jacket. His hair was black and curled around his face. His eyes were seeking but not for anything in particular. I met his kind gaze and he smiled. I fell instantly in love, worrying at the same time that I was trying to hold up my sister's bathing suit since it was at least two sizes too large.

I walked, with some grace I hoped, up the watery steps and out of the pool and grabbed a towel. We sat face-to-face on lounge chairs for quite a while. First we talked small talk, laughing how I had turned him down two nights earlier. I replied that it was safe now. The steamy nights we witnessed in the lobbies were over and my friend and I weren't here looking for that. He appeared hurt that I would think that of him, too, but he also smiled and laughed. I threw on my cover-up and we walked and talked some more about our respective lives, where we lived, what hobbies we enjoyed. When I returned for the final time to my hotel room, I re-dressed both literally and figuratively and went to meet this man for lunch.

My Adonis, whose name was William ("Will"), was a New York City firefighter working on a Bachelor's Degree in Economics, who read books and admired art. Will told me he wanted to buy artwork for his Brooklyn apartment and voila, there, in the lobby, was the inimitable Morris Katz, speed-painting with toilet paper; fake fine art. Will bought two of a series of three and I bought the third, an impulse buy that I could ill afford. Spun on a cotton candy cloud, I met my friends in the car at last minute departure and said: "That's the man I'm going to marry."

Moving back to New York meant being closer to my future husband and looking back now, the urgency seemed misguided but, well – extremely urgent. My new plan was to land a secretarial job at a major New York City corporation to pay for college courses. I would commute from a new apartment in New Rochelle, New York. One handy piece of depression-era advice my mother had given me was: "Ach! Learn how to type and you'll always have a job." Not only had I learned to type in high school, my typing speed was now a phenomenal 90+ words-a-minute as I had to write/type to meet the midnight deadline for the newspaper. I had also taken basic bookkeeping in high school and had office-temped during summers off; so I was ready to be a secretary. Or, so I thought.

I landed a job at Chase Manhattan Bank, Wall Street. I found a small studio apartment and could walk to the train station. Chase paid benefits and one could attend college and submit the bills. I could see my firefighter often without the long commute from South Jersey. From that moment on, I enjoyed a good run – still battling the anxiety attacks (running from work or school at times) and still working at 150% of my skill level to prove and maintain my worth at my job, but soon I won a promotion to secretarial supervisor, and, better yet, I had a loving, steady boyfriend.

After having primarily male friends at the newspaper and never quite fitting in with any group of young women, this almost guaranteed my utter failure at managing a group of "girly" girls whose main concerns were big hair, long manicured nails and dreams of tacky, glittery weddings to uneducated men. At home, I still had to eat a cheap diet of popcorn and spaghetti to survive. I longed for that perfect day when I could return to college full-time and earn my "real" job.

What I didn't realize at the time was that I was racking up business experience that was invaluable. While my peers were doing what I dreamed to do; attending college and partying without a care in the world and had all their bills paid, I earned bitter, hard-won stripes, work and real-life experience, and I increased my salary, bit by bit by bit.

I had just one year's worth of credit from NYU and was working to go to college. I was already leaving for work before the sun came up and coming home after dark. So I tried my hand at weekend-college, one three-credit course of intense study in management at Iona College. The professor, a working AT&T executive, offered me a job at month's end. "Thanks but no thanks," I said. "This is not my field of interest, or my dream." To challenge myself even further and for fun, I also took a chance on a tap dancing class. Alas, I had no talent to tap and my downstairs neighbors were not pleased.

The dream seemed to materialize when a new game came to town. Time, Incorporated decided to launch a TV-Guide type publication in the center of White Plains, the hub of Westchester. Dubbed 'TV-Cable Week,' it was intended to bring reverse commuting to Westchester for the first time. This was huge news. Big city folk were going to work here, most of them with reluctance, but the top editor already lived in the burbs and he typically achieved what he wanted, having launched People magazine to great success. I simply had to work there.

Little Carla was already 'temping' there and she was a great connection for me. I was granted an interview for an administrative position and, I took a day off work when I knew the phone call was supposed to come. I sat in my apartment and watched the 'pot' and waited for it to 'boil.' My Statue stood sentry, standing erect and intact. The phone finally rang and I did get the job. I was ecstatic and immediately began plotting how I would show the four Cable Week editors for whom I would work that I had real editorial experience; that I should be much more than an administrative employee – even though I did not have the usual college credentials.

This was another continuing theme, this proving "worthy" bit, because I didn't believe in myself. Morning after morning, I would still touch base with my Statue and wonder what I, a person who had no familial grounding whatsoever, had to offer the world as a valued contributor? My self-image was precarious at best; my self-doubt, immense. Underneath though, there lay a strong will and determination to prove myself wrong; to prove all of them wrong, even if I died trying.

One of my favorite pictures of "Little Carla," working for the Westchester County Executive's Office, New York; c1983.

Panic attacks, also known as anxiety attacks, are the number one reason people go to the emergency room thinking they're having a heart attack. Those of us who suffer such attacks understand this anomaly of the human "fight or flight" instinct. Slowly but surely, panic attacks, if misinterpreted, will turn into outright phobias as you try to avoid the situation that "caused" the panic attack. To this day, my attacks are random and without probable cause and I now know that experiencing panic attacks is an inherited trait. My mother, diagnosed with personality disorder in her late seventies, was also a severe agoraphobic which explains much of her behavior in my young life. Today, medications can ease the pain and suffering of those with this crippling disorder. Later, at age 24, I tackled the anxiety head on – never curing it, but learning to manage my panic attacks through a behavior modification program and good medications.

The terror that comes over me when the out of control feeling arises is all-consuming. The physical symptoms spiral and I throw up – a lot. The hell with my problems with my parents, I was using all my strength to work and go to school and hide this miserable problem that could rise up any time. I took trains, planes and automobiles home from various locations in the middle of an attack, to rush home to get to the bathroom and bed. I threw up in class, on the first day of a new job (right in the main office corridor), on the side of many a road, in numerous public restrooms, in airplanes, in the car, in my lap, at the rear of restaurants. I was always trying to beat the vomit home. For the next year or so, this was my existence – living independently but hustling to earn a college degree and work to the best of my ability; and suffering secret and frequent panic attacks.

For me, tackling a full-blown phobia required a Herculean effort but my growing career required it. I needed to travel, most often by company car, and getting stuck in traffic jams was so difficult I would map out many alternate routes before going anywhere. The effort to get to and from a meeting location and fulfill the requirements of the job at hand would leave me spent and exhausted, if I didn't have an anxiety attack and have to leave midway with many excuses.

In 1984, I applied and was accepted to the outstanding Phobia Clinic at White Plains Hospital Medical Center in White Plains, New York. An eight-week desensitization program taught me how to manage the panic using role-playing, brain games, a weekly support group, and actual forays into the real world with a trained aide by my side. I was honest with my employer and they assumed the cost. Difficult as it was, I completed the course and became a card-carrying member of the phobic's "club." They did actually issue you a yellow wallet card with the steps needed to talk yourself down from an attack.

I recall one young woman who was studying to become a pediatrician. She was terrified of balloons and couldn't walk into pediatric wards. Little by little, she learned how to be near a balloon, go on the rooftop with blown up balloons and watch them fly away and, finally, be near them when they popped. Phobias come in many shapes and sizes.

After eight weeks, I was ready to put what I learned to work and, although I did, a certain amount of armor remained in place to "protect and defend" me from the unnatural fight or flight response that characterizes agoraphobic behavior. It is described by The Mayo Clinic – the worldwide leader in medical care, research and education

– as "a type of anxiety disorder in which you avoid situations that you're afraid might cause you to panic." For example, some might avoid being alone, leaving home or entering any situation where they feel trapped, embarrassed or helpless if they do panic, particularly in crowded, public spaces.

Years later, strapped to a hospital bed in ICU, my very being became fight or flight. But there wasn't a thing I could do about the heart pounding, sweating, nausea, agitation, and downright fear, particularly when it came time to go home.

Chemotherapy x18

Finally, removing the tracheostomy tube and replacing it with a bandage/dressing that needed daily changing, the doctors gave me the go-ahead for outpatient treatment. I could go home and continue until I reached a total of 18 completed chemotherapy treatments.

My suit of armor was blown to bits and my Statue unrecognizable, dead in its dusty state. I couldn't even see its face. But I was home – free from the hospital for a time but also away from the safety of its nest. I didn't know what to do and neither did anyone else who was close to me. I couldn't think straight. I couldn't eat, take my medicines, walk, talk or, bathe without help. My children barely recognized me and were kept busy with school and activities with friends and family. I wrote things down furiously. Do this. Do that. Help me, please. My husband had to juggle it all including doling out carefully apportioned medications that were mysterious to me.

I felt awful. I looked awful, and it was only going to get worse as the chemotherapy "torture" continued. It was well into 1997 now and I had completely lost control both physically and mentally. Panic and anxiety came and went with such frequency that I felt that I was living one continuous attack. Now, that little yellow card from the phobia clinic was useless to me. Drugs helped quell the panic but sometimes the pain overrode the anxiety or added to the anxiety or vice-versa. I didn't know who I was.

I had unceasing heartburn. I developed vertigo. I ended up impacted with such severity that I was hospitalized just to relieve the constipation. I slept and woke never quite knowing where I was. I watched the O.J. Simpson travesty unfold on television and followed a trial I never would have even had on my radar before cancer. My husband, Will, started giving me Nupigen shots that a visiting nurse taught us how to do by injecting an orange. I took over and administered the shots myself, using the freckles on my legs as targets each day. The taste in my mouth was gun metal.

The chemo treatments were brutal. I awaited them like bomber jets as each one got worse. The effects were cumulative, I was told, and it was very true. I threw up constantly and watched the twisted carnage of the tracheotomy spot heal into a knot that impaired my swallowing. I listened to soft music. Happy, playful lyrics made me hate everyone. Longing, heartfelt lyrics made me love everyone. I hyperventilated and hallucinated. My mouth was so dry.

I emailed clients to inform them of my situation. The phone stopped ringing for work and rang only about illness. I didn't take any calls. I stopped walking because I couldn't walk anymore. I cried incessantly at home, at doctors' offices and when I had to stay at the hospital again. 'I am alive and fighting,' I repeated over and over to myself. 'I am alive and fighting.'

The chemotherapy ward was both my savior and my enemy. With loud protest, I was taken there by my husband and endured the six hours of dripping poison. Most of the medicines were clear or a fuzzy white, but one was a bright red that was so unnatural in color, I will remember it all my life. The smell of the hospital's Dial© soap alone could make me gag; the familiar phone ring instills panic. Separated by curtains from other patients being similarly treated, murmurs of consolation were offered up by both nurses and relatives in aid. Occasionally, a doctor wandered in to check up or give news – either good or bad. Sometimes I heard cheers, other times, sobs.

Chemotherapy and IV nurses are specially trained and a gift to cancer patients. Their competence and caring is unrivaled. I can't recall any of their names, but I do remember how swift and efficient they were; how tuned in to each and every patient's needs. My cries of protest and tears were never met with annoyance or anger. More often, they apologized to me for the pain and discomfort they were about to inflict. I marveled at their goodness even though most of the time, I didn't even understand what was going on medically.

Many times, I would go straight from the chemo ward into the hospital because I suffered dire side effects. Other times, I was astonished when I was allowed to simply leave and be poured back into the car, somehow getting home and into bed. I thought a lot about my bruised childhood and wondered how I ended up here, now. I also liked to imagine being at my desk, working, chatting up my clients; creating. I liked to think that I would return to that life someday.

Back in the hospital, I questioned just how many transfusions can one body take? I was curious to know so I finally asked one of the nurses while the blood or platelets were dripping in through my port. "As many as you need, honey," she said. "As many as you need." I wondered why she was sitting there, crouched on the floor. So I asked her and she told me that allergic reactions to blood products could occur at any time therefore the transfusion nurse was required to sit with you through the entire process. Scared, I turned away and went back to my own thoughts as she bantered with incoming and outgoing doctors and nurses in my private room.

I was still afraid. I shuddered with fear as I heard the machine infusing me with what could possibly – only possibly – reverse my chemo wipeout, a devastating side effect of chemotherapy that kills all of your good white cells and platelets as well as the deadly cancerous ones. I tried to remember if this was my second or third chemo wipeout. I didn't remember. But I did know if my body didn't regenerate cells on its own after the transfusions, I was done. "There is nothing else I can do," I recall my oncologist saying. So, I waited and pondered.

Months into chemotherapy now, I thought about my doctors, the good, bad and ugly. I remembered one who came to see me after the first tumor biopsy and, in my drug daze connected to the noisy lung machine, I smiled and remarked happily: "You came to see me." She replied, "Yes," and did a perfunctory check of my chart and patted my hand. I had seen this rheumatologist only once and both she and I knew I would never see her again since my care had been transferred to a new group and hospital. Again, I smiled as she left thinking she cared enough just to check on me. Months later, I saw her bill for the visit. The joke was on me.

I thought about the dueling cardio-thoracic surgeons and grew confused and angry as I realized my first post-operative visit did not go well. One week after discharge from the mediastinal biopsy hospital stay, I revisited the Stan and Laurel of surgery and was asked, "Where are your x-rays? I said: "What x–rays?" I was informed that I was supposed to have had a post-op x-ray of my lungs to see if fluid was filling or had stayed drained. I knew of no such request. The doctors shrugged it off and sent me on my way. I wondered if that x-ray could have revealed the swelling that caused the emergency tracheotomy. I wondered but still didn't question.

I smiled when I thought of my very diligent oncologist from Sloan Kettering who arrived with regularity, genuinely concerned for my well-being. I could tell by her furrowed brow and the way she fluttered her fingertips on her lips: She cared. I grew concerned when those hot-to-the-touch, red dollar coin-sized blotches appeared on my stomach and arms. No infectious disease or other medical specialist could discern what was causing crop circles to form on my person. A dermatologist was called in for a biopsy. He botched it by informing me that he did not take enough tissue for an accurate diagnosis. It took a year before the blotches faded into a light tan and then disappeared completely a full second year later. No one could ever explain what they were.

I was an oddity or "unusual case" as I heard over and over again; I saw nearly every specialist of every type and had test after test. I didn't know why but I still didn't question. I was in their hands and, regardless of my bad experiences, I still trusted. I had CT scans, MRIs, muga scans, Gallian scans and PT scans repeatedly and fell asleep in many of the testing machines

The cardiologists who followed the ambulance to the Medical Center on that snowy January 5th visited often, too. They never did that before for a patient, they exclaimed, and were grateful for the positive outcome. They were as puzzled as I was about what happened

94

but determined to see me through my ordeal. I thanked them and still hold them dear.

Three years later, as my brain cleared and I sorted through what did happen to me by asking questions of family, friends and doctors, listening to all their responses very carefully. I realized, with a bit of horror, that many mistakes were made by the medical community, including physicians, nurses, technicians, and hospital staff. A few of these doctors remain my heroes and I am forever indebted to their due diligence. The others, I understand, were simply human. However, it was hard to learn that iconic figures disappoint and screw up. Still very much the distrustful child, I did start trying to put back on that lifelong protective armor but there was no Amy Statue to armor. I was still goop.

The Doctor Dilemma

When you're goop, you are extremely vulnerable. Your thinking is clouded and you must leave all decisions up to others. The mistakes and outright catastrophes that occurred with my medical care are simply disgraceful. I became aware of hospitals' "Monday Morning Meetings" (now the title of a fictional television show that portrays doctors reviewing peer errors) and I still wish physicians could utter those two words many patients need to hear: "I'm sorry."

But then and, most likely, still today, that is next to impossible with medical malpractice costs and the quicksand of our national, semi-privatized medical care system. I was clueless when it came to who held responsibility for the mangled lump I had become and, ruefully, it was clear that some doctors participate in the cover up for their friends. I would be remiss if I did not clearly state that missing my diagnosis of Stage 4B cancer for a very long period of time was and will be forevermore my family physician's mistake.

According to a study referenced by CNN, "medical errors kill more than a quarter million people every year in the United States and injure millions. Add them all up and 'you have probably the third leading cause of death' in the country, says Dr. Peter Pronovost, an anesthesiologist and critical care physician at Johns Hopkins Hospital." [2] This does not promote confidence. Nor does it provide an answer except that a patient must be his or her best advocate and if the patient cannot fulfill that role, a family member or trusted friend must step in.

Other than hollering at the doctors, nurses or other attendants in both hospitals and private offices, what is a patient to do? I have concluded that we and our advocates must scream – loudly and often. Doctors frequently are asked by women: "Would your treatment plan be any different if I was your sister, mother or wife? I believe they've

---

[2] The Gruesome Math of Hospital Infections; CNN.com; April 14th, 2011

become immune to that query and say 'yes' by rote. Bringing a list of questions is good as well as a pad of paper and pen to take notes. Sounds too simple? For some, it is a very difficult process. Unfortunately, now I've had years of practice.

In the years since my initial diagnoses, I have shouted, argued written letters, thrown things, cursed, and finally relied on introducing myself to any new physician in any specialty with a sheaf of papers that detail my medical history in chronological order plus a list of all my treating doctors including telephone numbers and my medications plus dosage. I say very clearly: *"I have a very complicated medical history. I understand if you cannot or do not care to treat me but please be honest and up front and I will go elsewhere."* Some have been honest and immediately referred me to a more knowledgeable and/or compassionate colleague and others have foolhardily taken me into their exam room and proceeded to perform an exam, ask questions and then chastise and criticize me about my myriad of ills when I specifically asked them not to do that. Then they hear some choice words and the door slamming behind me on my way out.

I have written an 'open letter' to doctors that I share here. I wish it was required reading for all in the medical community. Angry? Yes. Frustrated? Even more so. However, the dozen or so specialists and primary care doctors that I have amassed over the years who now treat me and my multiple conditions are the cream of the crop. They didn't turn me away and it took me a long time to find them.

Dear Doctor:

I don't feel well and am suffering most of the time. My conditions seem to be winning the war and the medications are causing side effects that can, sometimes, be intolerable. I am not stressed out (other than worrying about my illnesses) nor am I hormonal or a hypochondriac and it's not 'all in my head.' I am truly in distress.

While prescribing medications including steroids may work in the short-term, it is unreasonable to expect me to take high doses for a long period of time during which I will undoubtedly experience side effects. I need a treatment plan that looks at the whole me – all of what my physical body has been through, the side effects of the medications you and other doctors have prescribed, and how my mental health is affected as well. This is what I call true integrative medicine.

I know treating people with multiple disorders is more an art than an exact science but I am asking that you listen to me as often as I need you to hear what I have to say. I am asking that you keep an open mind while also remembering any medical trends you might have recorded about me during my care. I am asking that you keep current on research or studies that might help me. I am asking that you understand that I am not asking for a miracle, just a cure, if one is available, or relief that will last for a time. And when that course of action doesn't work anymore, you adjust with the utmost of care.

In turn, I promise to always bring you updated lists of my medications, hospitalizations and procedures as well as results of any lab work. I will be faithful to the regimen you prescribe unless I have concerns and then I will let you know immediately. I will not have you paged unless it is a true emergency. I will respect you and your staff's time.

I'm having a really hard time with all of this and need you, most of all, to be on my side. I appreciate all that you do and look forward to continuing to work with you.

With my thanks,

Your Patient

Integrative Medicine Specialist Dalal Akoury, M.D. of Myrtle Beach, South Carolina says we are the chief executive officers of our own health. She feels that the most important thing physicians can do is "get back to understanding that we are healers" and not pharmaceutical or insurance company representatives. In fact, she feels so strongly about the impact that pharmaceutical firms have had on health care today, she is not optimistic about our current president's idea of a hybrid of socialized medicine that will give us less choices rather than more.

Dr. Akoury's AwareMed [3] practice and national groups like the Institute for Functional Medicine are quite clear when they explain how we at a crossroads in medical care; as the population ages and lives longer and care options become broader but restrictions become tighter:

"We are in the midst of an epidemic of chronic disease that threatens the health of our people and the economic well-being of our nation. Systems-based care and strong therapeutic partnerships are required to address the dysfunctions that arise when genetic susceptibility, environmental exposures, and unhealthy lifestyles intersect—as they do in varying ways for most people. Functional medicine is designed to meet just this challenge—to help practitioners and patients recognize, manage, and prevent the interconnected web of dysfunction that is at the foundation of chronic disease."

With offices in Washington and New Mexico, the Institute informs us that "more than 100,000 practitioners from 73 countries have been introduced to the principles and practices of functional medicine" through their conferences as well as those of similar organizations. Clearly, the medical community is interested.

Other like-minded and far reaching organizations that promote integrative medicine are the American College for Advancement in Medicine based in California and the Society for Integrative Oncology that offers many webinars as well as onsite conferences. Sponsored by both traditional medical facilities, such as the Dana Farber Cancer Institute in Massachusetts, and The Weil Foundation in Arizona, among others, the Society is on the cutting edge of what is new and what works – well. Just a mere 20 years ago, no one could have imagined that these diverse thinkers could converge and create a movement to change the universal model of medical practice to one that integrates all the fantastic knowledge within Eastern/Western, alternative/traditional, holistic/specialty knowledge held by these bodies and others.

---

[3] http://www.awaremedonline.com/aboutus.asp

The Brooklyn Alphabet

Almost simultaneously back in 1983, my dream man and I decided to get married and my mother informed me of a clause in her divorce decree from my father that dictated that I was to get $10,000 upon turning age 18. Now 23, I decided it was time to collect. I had no job, no degree and was planning to get married. Surely, he couldn't, wouldn't deny me this? The irony was not lost on me that I would have to attack the first major male figure in my life while seeking to cleave myself to the next.

On a shoestring budget, Will and I get married; September 15, 1984.

I went to family court and met with two county lawyers who, when I recounted my tale of woeful parental negligence, advised that I sue my father for the financial support that he should have legally provided me, including college funds. It didn't matter, they said, whether he had the money or not. If he was working, he would be dunned for it. They also asked me several times how, a person such as me, who had suffered such, was not a drug addict, in the gutter, or seeking to kill myself. I replied that I had never even thought of such things and if there was a cartoon balloon over my head it would have said: "Huh?"

Shortly thereafter, my derelict father received a subpoena and I received a phone call. We met. I wept and decided I couldn't go through with it. It was not worth the emotional pain that would most certainly send me backward rather than the tentative forward I had managed. We negotiated. I mentioned the $10,000. He gave me $5,000. This, then, was my share of a down payment on a co-op my future husband and I bought. Will was 'da brains' from Brooklyn and became my stability even though he used the Brooklyn alphabet frequently; 'eff–ing A,' 'eff–ing B,' 'eff–ing C,' etc. Attached to him with a huge invisible bungee cord, I could fling myself out to the farthest reaches of my gall and reap high-risk rewards.

As "the stable one," William Louis Santagata, Jr. was all I could have ever wanted. Handsome, strong, smart, funny and good with money; I fell hard for him. His face was manly — with stubble at times — yet just as soft. His light brown eyes took a slight, soothing downturn at the right of each eyelid, a family trait inherited from his mother. Those eyes, coupled with his lips — especially when curled into a sly smile – drew me to fall into his soul.

Also endearing was his love and loyalty to his sister's two sons, Richie and John. As John's father was around and Richie's was not, Will assumed the father role toward Richie with such tender loving care. I was eager to understand a man who had this inbred devotion, as his own childhood could be described as more horrific than mine. While the ills of his youth were easier to understand — the early death of his mother and the alcoholic aftermath of his father, the pain he bore yet overcame to father a fatherless boy amazed me. Because his early life included more easily understood reasons for him to forge his own path, his history made me more determined to understand my own still-to-be deciphered motives.

Nephews Richie (left) and John with our dog, Kingsley c1985.

Our young, forced independence was a strong common bond. Years later, we would remark that at least one of us should have married into an extended family of normalcy and wealth as we plodded along and made good, solid life decisions. We were madly in love and we made it work, marrying in 1984 in a small ceremony and reception we paid for with the gifts received – a complete wash including a modest honeymoon. My parents attended and, to my astonishment, actually sat next to each other in the front row, a shock I absorbed as I walked, alone head held high down the "aisle" in the restaurant. I would not allow anyone to "give me away." Will was 28, I was 24 and our relationship had been forged without any kind of roadmap. He accepted me for the best of it and the rest of it. I was blessed.

Also, I was euphoric about my work at TV-Cable Week, a Time, Inc. magazine, and my life with Will. I did prove myself and was proclaimed "the best damned channel editor of the lot" by a grizzled editor who every week found himself producing a new magazine from scratch. As a "channel editor," I edited thousands of "vanilla" television listings for all the TV stations in the country and adapted them to Time, Inc. style. Creative and satisfying, I sat side-by-side with college graduates who earned up to $6,000 more than I did but I was the best, because I could produce more copy with fewer errors faster than the rest. We wrote and edited at warp speed. We helped research 'wrap' stories. I remember the aura of walking into a real writer's office and being given the privilege of helping research the celebrity of the day. I loved my boss. I loved the people, the place. I could work 12 to 20 hours and not feel it at all.

We enjoyed perks I had never known – free magazines, cable TV, movie premieres, a shower and kitchen, cots for sleep, luncheons, and the company of intelligent people. We could laugh together and, ultimately, cry together when, six months later, the magazine folded. "But they promised us three years," I wailed to no one in particular. A wise older editor put her arm around me and said: "Everything will be okay." But it wasn't okay; not with me. I would have to dust my crackled Statue off and rise yet again.

Time, Inc. management offered us employment counseling and a percentage of our salaries for training in any field. My percentage was low. It paid for bartender's school. 'Why not,' I figured. 'I would at least be able to post my sorry self behind a counter and share sob stories with other failures.' The only difference being they would be drunk and I wouldn't be. Other TV-Cable Week refugees were offered jobs at the still successful Time, Inc. city-based publications and went on to write books. My boss interviewed me at a mall cafeteria some months later as he wrote his tome about the TV-Cable Week debacle: The Fanciest Dive,[4] a sorry read, even today.

Twenty-five years later, looking at the swift decline and fall, I am reminded of the ill-fated business decisions banks made in the '90s and first decade of the 21st century – a Ponzi scheme built without oversight or financing. However, this was an editorial collapse of Biblical proportions for Time and the corporation. The end was abrupt and left the colossal office edifice in White Plains with pock-marked walls that were never painted; spiral staircases forever unfinished: Time just up and left, declaring an early defeat. My funniest/fondest memory is when my computer started smoking and caught fire, as I typed furiously to meet deadlines that didn't even matter. They called

---

[4] The Fanciest Dive: What Happened When the Giant Media Empire of Time/Life Leaped Without Looking into the Age of High-Tech; Christopher M. Byron; W W Norton & Co Inc; 1 edition (February 1986)

for the tech crew but no one thought to look for a fire extinguisher, except me, and in the building's unfinished glory, I couldn't find one.

"So, that's that," said Pooh. What do we do next?"

At this interval, I had to use my father's name and credentials as a "namedrop" at the next job interviews. Selling out, as they say, from journalism to public relations, I answered an ad for a public relations and special events coordinator at a not-for-profit agency. My father was a noteworthy and accomplished practitioner in that field and his name was known throughout the public relations and fundraising industries. In fact, he was deemed the renowned creator of direct mail fundraising and it certainly helped that I was trained at his knee in some of the fine arts of fundraising, including clear-cut deception such as the use of my crying baby photo in the Care appeal and his fundraising letters signed off by "Ham Jordan" of the Jimmy Carter campaign. I brought copies of both to the interview. Of course, my potential employers would not know we were estranged and, I am sure, thought they could get a free benefit; advice from my father, the guru, through me, which did not ever happen.

Hired, I settled into a job I hated – and that paid little – while I sought to continue my college education. I was working with a gaggle of women; an arena I already knew was not my forte. But I powered up and worked at my intense pace, volunteering for every task no one else wanted. I put together the first personal computers to arrive at the office, gleeful when the initial control prompt in the DOS operating system actually appeared. I also ran existing fundraising events and created new ones. I drove all over the county soliciting participants in whatever "thon" of the day we were doing. I worked for a County chapter of the American Heart Association so there was certainly some cache in being a part of a national force when I had resources for learning that stretched far beyond our little office.

All the while, I thought of what my next job would be and succeeded in alienating almost everyone in the office. Yet I produced some of my best work. I was asked to participate in a media relations panel at PACE University, White Plains, New York, and did so with great acclaim from the participants and scholarly organizer. To this day, I cherish his letter of praise. It was my "hah!" to the world that a non-college graduate could be recognized by an institution of higher learning. My measly salary was supplemented by bartending once or twice a week. Those 9 a.m. to midnight days would end at home with or without Will, depending on whether or not he was working at the firehouse, and with a shot of vodka to help me sleep. The bartender drinks!

I enrolled in Empire State College, an independent study school that is part of the State University of New York (SUNY). Once again, I was told my work was "genius" but I wondered when the acclaim I kept receiving would result in some sort of payoff rather than extremely hard work. And, I believed I was in control.

I wasn't going to get an honorary degree from any college so I just kept working and going to my independent study college sessions and tending our little co-op. We turned that baby around for a quick profit and used the proceeds for a down payment on a small ranch home in Ossining, New York. Yes, the "Ossining" – home of the famous Sing Sing prison where local lore says every home's lights dimmed when Old Sparky jolted another death row inmate. I still joke that I check in "up the river" every evening at 6:00 sharp.

The grim history of Sing Sing overrides such humor. The reality of our imposing neighbor, where Ethel and Julius Rosenberg were executed, was threatening. I learned as much about its history as I could. I also learned that prison escapees typically headed for the train station south to Manhattan; and that's exactly what happened the several times inmates escaped while we continued to live in Ossining.

Will and I trying to make "The American Dream" work; 1986.

We were living the American dream and in order to do so, I needed to land yet another job for more money. I promptly did get hired at a nationwide private water utility. I finally earned a title and a big office with a window in upscale Greenwich, Connecticut. Oh what a life – filled with a decent salary, a company car, new challenges, expanded learning opportunities and, again, hard, hard labor. Thrust back into my comfortable world of men, my job description was so intense I felt like I had multiple personality disorder. Reading it today I am aghast at how many hats I wore and how much I did to remain worthy yet again.

Two more anvils would fall on my head during this time; the first, the unforeseen death of my husband's dear nephew, Richie, at age 15. As I had joined Will's Italian famiglia, I, too, showered his sister's two boys with love, bought clothes, welcomed them into our home on all school vacations, loved them as my own, and went along with the expenditures we made to help my husband's "other family in Long Island" live well. Richie didn't resemble Will much except for the same down-turned eyelids. He had light brown hair and was very bright and capable. He and Will shared a love of baseball, a game Will taught him in Richie's own backyard. Loving and kind, Richie never

106

said a bad word about anyone that I can recall, even his stepfather who had ignored him.

Just one week before I started work at the water company, Richie died. His demise was due to a congenital immune deficiency to which he succumbed after a series of seemingly benign respiratory infections. I cried on my way to and from work for a month. It was another early death for my husband to overcome and he slid into a deep grief which would last almost three years and almost unraveled our marriage. There was simply no antidote to the loss of a child and those first months without Richie were excruciating. As Christmas neared, we bought a small, live evergreen and planted it behind our house. Today, it stands almost 60 feet tall, a testament to the great man Richie most certainly would have become.

The other Wiley Coyote anvil came relatively soon afterwards. My husband and I decided to have a baby. Having suffered from ovarian cysts and several minor surgeries for endometriosis and the like during my teens to my early '20s, I was told I would have trouble conceiving. And so I did. But we persevered with the right doctors and treatments and – surprise – I was pregnant! It was a tentative pregnancy as earlier in our marriage I lost two pregnancies, miscarrying in the first trimester.

During my sixth month of pregnancy, I left the water company to start my own business. And, on his due date, November 28, 1989, Daniel Richard Santagata was born, the happiest day of my life. Oh, how I loved being a mother. Daniel had insatiable desire for fun, love, and wild activity. And I was gleeful to satisfy his every need. Unfettered, we would go-go-go, giggle, play, cuddle and communicate on a new, uniquely deep level. This is also when I decided not to deny Daniel his grandparents, my own parents. I resumed a dialogue with my each of them.

However, as many of my readers of the 1970's women's liberation generation will know, delaying pregnancy and the resulting infertility is one of the most emotionally painful trials couples can endure. If you are lucky enough to come out on the other end, you have earned a special badge, joined a club you never wanted to join, and will look at all children as miracles. Daniel certainly was our miracle and we prayed to Richie that Daniel would honor his memory with his middle name. After a true loving bond developed between my Dad and Daniel, it was also fitting that his middle name was also my father's.

Telecommuting was just becoming known and my first clients were privately-held water utilities throughout the country, including the two divisions I had left. Within a few short months, I had a very young baby, a great nearby babysitter and a home office. I thought business would grow slowly; it skyrocketed. Just three weeks after Daniel was born, I was writing and producing a video.

As every working mother knows, juggling schedules, responsibilities and priorities can turn into one big mud trough. Just as soon as you pull things out, other things get sucked into the vortex. Add John, (Richie's younger, half-brother) a troubled adolescent to the mix and – well, let's just say I didn't know where I was going until I hopped in my car and looked at my calendar. When Daniel was only 10 months old, John came to live with us, destroyed by the death of his brother and his mother's inability to care for him. My husband assumed guardianship and I found myself the instant mother of a toddler and a teenager as well as sole proprietor of a thriving business. I also began having an insuppressible cough.

The ghost Richie visited us several times the first year after his death. My most vivid encounter occurred when I was dozing on the living room couch, TV on, Will at work. I woke to the sounds of our large Shepherd-Collie-Husky mix whimpering in his sleep. Looking over, I noticed his fur rippling. I could smell Richie before I felt him. The house had an odor I'd never experienced. I felt so at peace and told Richie that his dear uncle was at the firehouse and he should go visit him there. The smell faded and I fell back into a glorious sleep. After that night, I started researching life after death, old souls versus new souls, and visitations from beyond, and I learned enough to say with confidence that Richie had been there, though I know many people would dispute such visitations.

To say that these were happy, worrisome, crazy, stress-filled times is an understatement. I recall two high (or low) points that drove my future work life decision-making. One, I was moving a load of laundry downstairs where John had made his bedroom on our pull-out couch and I lay down for a moment and fell fast asleep, still holding the laundry basket for at least two hours. Awakening, I saw my Statue and it had cracked down the middle. The omen struck me. Deep inside, I may have known then, my life was in danger.

But there was also the other moment, charged with hope within chaos. I was home after a day's client work, having recently hooked up with a partner thinking two could handle this business better than one. (It was another "am I worthy just to be me?" moment and I needed the bolster of a seasoned professional.) He anointed me Vice President of his small, very successful agency and, together, we accomplished great things. On the phone with my new partner, I was standing at the stove, frying fish, alternating between pen and spatula while editing a grease-splattered manuscript on the counter. Daniel clung to my leg for dear life, crying for his bottle. I lost it, but in a good way. I became hysterical – laughing, laughing, laughing. I could bring home the bacon, fry it up in a pan…oh forget it!!! This was hopeless!! I hung up the phone, turned off the stove, and tended to the real priority – Daniel. All else could wait.

John stayed with us for a little more than three years. I am proud to say we helped him make the life decisions that sent him on his way to a successful career as a chef. Unfortunately, in his late 20's, John would be diagnosed with a serious mental illness which overwhelmed him. A loving man to the day he died at age 35 of a heart attack, John was always haunted by his own childhood demons (including the tragic deaths of both his brother, Richie, and his own estranged father in a house fire). We didn't see him often enough once he left our home. Daniel and his later-to-be brother, Brett, remember John simply as "E." John would arise from sleep and open the basement door and say "Ayyyyyy" in Fonzie-like tone. The children interpreted this as "E." We all still refer to him as "E" and we miss him terribly.

Nephew John and our son, Daniel c1991.

After John moved on, Will and I tried for a second baby. It was not to be and, much later, I learned it was likely because cancer was already growing and my immune system was going into overdrive to protect me from its wrath. But, as it is written somewhere in God's sky, I had always wanted to have one biological child and adopt a second child. Not wanting, or being able to afford a baby through traditional adoptions of the day whether domestic or foreign, we explored the idea of becoming foster parents. Perhaps if the 1990's children's services programs were in place when Will and I were young, we might have been removed from our respective homes.

It was our calling, we said, to give foster parenting a try. I put aside my continued coughing and other vague symptoms of illness, attributing them to stress. After completing our certification course and home study, we waited for a phone call. One interesting aspect to applying for a foster child is that you can ask for a specific age. I found it scary that one woman in our training class wanted a teen so she could have someone to go with her to the movies. We weren't in it for that, nor did we realize there was any compensation for taking in foster children. We forged ahead.

Daniel was then coming fast upon age six and our only reservations were that the child not be of any danger to Daniel. Thus, we asked for children under the age of two. We missed a few calls for babies (cell phones were not popular yet) and then at my Church one Sunday in September 1995 at a particularly moving service, I prayed that the child who was meant to be with us – even if for just a short while – would present him/herself soon.

Welcome Brett! On October 5, 1995 the call came. Brett was a little over two years old, malnourished, ill, and needed a home, at least for three months. He weighed barely 19 pounds, had a distended tummy and needed mucho food and even more love. But he was also a little love bug and, from the first day, bopped around our house, in between monitored and measured feedings, saying "Hellooo. Hellooo. Hellooo." We watched and waited and Brett, very soon, adopted us – turning away from his biological mother on enforced visits, which suggested there was much more to that relationship beneath the surface.

In a year, he grew four inches and met all physical and mental standards for his chronological age. Daniel and Brett grew very close. Often, we would find Brett's crib empty in the morning and he would be curled up with Daniel in his big-boy bed. The three months passed and stretched into years and on September 26, 2000 at age seven, Brett David Santagata was adopted. It was the second happiest day of my life! Of course, there is much more to this story, dear readers, but that is Brett's story, not mine; however intricately entwined we are.

If anything defined "normal" in my mind, it was the idea that we had done this – that our little family was complete. We were "normal." We were a real nuclear family of four with a modest house, two cars and two careers. In the years leading up to his formal adoption, little Brett proved to be a miraculous gift. He was funny, smart, and loved to live in our laps. We learned that he had actually spent the first nine months of his life with a wonderful abuela in South America. It was clear that she had given him that early bonding experience and a loving spirit. We just had to recapture that capacity to love and he was ours.

Around this time, I remember having a play date with a friend who said that she had already decided what her son was going to be when he grew up. Quizzically, I tried to process what she was saying. An architect, she proclaimed. What did I want my boys to be, she asked? I thought for a moment as I had never had a thought like that before, and replied: "Kind and wise. That's it. Kind and wise." She looked at me askance and we went on with merry boy play.

Brett's arrival in 1995 was the beginning of an unparalleled chapter in my own life – I finally had joined the ranks of the normal – but the reprieve lasted for an extremely brief time. On the surface, I was managing and enjoying my life, although I was more frantic than ever. In secret, I suffered – a daily vision of my Statue crumbling under its own weight. I was coughing, short of breath, having fevers and night sweats. My body was failing and I sensed I must mend my cracked Statue, or crumble. What followed was the battle – life against death, well-being versus excruciating disease.

Hand Wringers, Pity People and God

'Oh, what to do; what to do.' I wrung my hands with worry and lay in pain and panic. Perhaps I was at treatment number 12 or 13 or maybe even 14. I had lost count. The mouth sores prevented me from eating but the steroids made me ravenous. I sucked down Carnation instant breakfast and ate Swanson turkey TV dinners that gave me a memory of childhood comfort in the beginning but were now just sustenance. Nothing tasted right.

Once, I craved popcorn and ate a whole bowl. Within 15 minutes, I was in excruciating pain with heartburn. I used a hot water bottle and sat ramrod straight in the bed rocking back and forth through the night. I don't know where my husband slept. I anticipated that he was with one or both of the boys, helping calm them through the night as I moaned or cried out in pain. I longed to be with them but could only wrestle with my distorted thoughts. I now had "chemo brain," a condition that caused confusion and delirium. I had trouble speaking and understanding those who spoke to me. I just followed the protocol. Followed the protocol.

One night, I was feverish and unable to move. Will argued with me about going to the hospital. 'I can't go,' I thought. 'Leave me be.' Somehow, he wrestled me into the car, neighbors were called to watch the boys, and off we went – back to a place I dreaded but also thought of as refuge. With warmed blankets, the nurses welcomed me. My spent husband left, knowing that I was in good care. I sank into stupor and let them do what they had to do. I didn't even care anymore.

Yet another night, I was in such terrible pain while hospitalized that I begged to see my rheumatologist who monitored the steroids that were given me on top of the Prednisone and Decadron that are part of my chemotherapy. It was midnight when he arrived and, as I pled for help, he explained that he could give me Solumetrol for the pain but, if he did, it would break both of my hips. I recoiled and sank further into the bed. Thanks but no thanks. He left. I continued to cry in pain and somehow managed. Somehow.

I knew I was nearing the end, one way or the other. Either my chemo would be done and the seemingly bottomless pit would seal, or I would die. I didn't want to die like that – in that ugly, weakened, tortured state, I thought. I couldn't believe it myself, but I still didn't want to die.

Carrying on (or being carried on), I was buoyed soon after to learn that I was in remission at treatment number 14. Sloan protocol only called for two more treatments after remission is reached. Therefore, I was spared two of Sloan protocol's 18 treatments. Looming were treatments 15 and 16, the worst ever.

It was summer 1997 and I braced myself for the end. In constant pain, I let the chemo nurses hook me up for number 15. Will was with me and I threw up as soon as the drip started. The retching continued the entire six hours. I slept some but vomited more. I don't recall going home. I do recall throwing up for two more weeks and running a gauntlet of blood tests and shots.

My brother, Steve, took me to my final treatment in August. Will was at work. Again, I threw up the entire time but was determined now to see it through to the end. I had come this far, what else could possibly happen? Nothing – and I went home with cheers from the nurses and vomit spittle on my face. I smiled a crooked smile and said goodbye. I secretly vowed never to be back.

As I recalled, the director of the Sloan Kettering unit where I was treated said. "Get ready for nine months of torture." Even though nine months extended into 12 because of my many complications, I didn't know that much, much later, I would thank him for his honesty. Because of the countless times when I never left the chemo department to go back "home," I found room 201C South in solitary where the nurses knew me and my tendency for always feeling shivering cold, a place of comfort. Later, I would be diagnosed with post-traumatic stress disorder (PTSD) that required intensive psychotherapy and serotonin uptake medications similar to Prozac.

PTSD is most commonly familiar when applied to war survivors or crime victims or the unpredictably bereaved through natural or human or property disasters. However, trauma is trauma. Clinically, it's described as "an anxiety disorder that some people get after seeing or living through a dangerous event. When in danger, it's natural to feel afraid. This fear triggers many split-second changes in the body to prepare to defend against the danger or to avoid it. This "fight-or-flight" response is a healthy reaction meant to protect a person from harm. But in PTSD, this reaction is changed or damaged. People who have PTSD may feel stressed or frightened even when they're no longer in danger."

Already being treated ever since I was a child for generalized anxiety disorder, this event surely put me over the edge, enough so that, often, I questioned my sanity or my future ability to become sane again.

I set up a categorization system for people who visited. There were the Hand Wringers who were amazed I was alive and gave dire predictions for my future. I met the Pity People, those who felt sorry for me and would pat me on the head, an infuriating gesture, and suggest therapy ('I can't walk or talk but bring me the best!'). "That which doesn't kill us only makes us stronger," many said. ('Screw that!') And, best of all, those who preached that God only gives you what you can handle. ('Oh really? Is that your God or my God?')

Finally, there were the Vanishers, those people who can't handle critical illness, cancer, death or dying in any form. It was quite jarring to realize I would never hear from certain friends or business associates again. But flowers were delivered and promptly removed (no plants or flowers around an immune-compromised person), meals came by barge, it seemed, as my Church rallied and members arrived bearing huge amounts of consumable goods. At one count, we had 12 meat loaves in our freezer. It was good food for family and visitors. I couldn't eat any of it.

When I wasn't throwing up, I subsisted on the instant breakfast drinks, French toast, and those turkey TV dinners that was mushy and tasty, to me. I longed for my mother's mashed potatoes and My-T-Fine Chocolate pudding that would have skin on top after refrigerated. I wanted to just lick the spoons, but when I thought of her "secret ingredient," the ashes from her ever-present cigarette that would fall into whatever pot her good cooking simmered in, I thought better of asking her for those spoons.

My father returned from vacation. As some sort of penance, he appeared almost every day to care for me. When the children were in school, I would moan or cry out for anyone who was in the house and many times it was my Dad, with sad eyes and soft hands, laying heating pads or ice packs where I needed them or bringing me water to take my pills. It was quite astonishing, really, to think his third wife allowed him this time with me. And, with weariness and wariness, I permitted myself to be Daddy's little girl.

Most often, while I longed for him to sing out: "Amy Sue, where are you?" he was silent and gentle when handling me. I think he was probably scared to death to think of the unthinkable (losing his youngest) but his World War II Army medic training took over and I did feel his love.

Dad and I during happier times on a mesa in New Mexico where I accompanied him on a business trip; 1972.

My agoraphobic mother — who seldom left her bedroom — actually journeyed the 30 miles by taxi from Mamaroneck to visit me.

It was a tense visit and, mostly, she cried. She also repeated: "Nem too dawm. Nem too dawm," Hungarian for it's going to be okay. She was gone before I knew it (I think I fell asleep from the Hungarian keening of "Nem too dawm"), and we agreed later to communicate by cards, letters and phone, a promise she did keep.

After the first two months of crisis treatment, a schedule was created to allow my husband to return to work. The shifts alternated, amongst siblings, neighbors and friends – some of whom would sleep over to take care of my little boys and look in on me when Will had to work the night shift. Many of those nights and other days, I wound up in an ambulance and back at the hospital. When Will wasn't home, I became scared and agitated. Soon enough, the others stopped telling me when he left.

And, in the early weeks of chemo, there was the daily change of bandages on the tracheotomy site. A nurse friend assisted. Nothing worked. Ripping that bandage off and leaving me without a way to breathe ('OH NO, PLEASE, NO!!'), cleaning it with Betadyne (felt like acid) and putting on new bandages would not allow the wound to heal. After many inquiries, my husband found a unique kind of transparent, waterproof bandage that could stay put until the damn thing healed; something that should have taken a few days, took months because of the anti-healing effects of the chemo.

It would be nearly two years before I could have the twisted leftover carnage of the emergency tracheotomy repaired in a reconstructive surgery during which I had to be awake throughout ('HELP ME,' my voiceless voice screamed!) as I heard every noise in the operating room including a loud crash that turned out to be a pregnant nurse fainting.

I blew up from my incredible doses of steroids. I felt like The Incredible Hulk and looked like him too except I wasn't green and I was bald. Cushings Syndrome (increased weight and body bloat from high doses of steroids) also hurts like hell. I had a double port that had been surgically implanted on my upper left chest. I can barely remember that surgery. I was told it should normally be on the right, but there had been other inserted tubes and things there, so it was there on the left. There was no numbing cream then. Pain became Amy. Amy became pain. No one, except my children, escaped my wrath whether I croaked it out or wrote it out. I was angry at the world and the doctor who missed my diagnosis, my keepers, and whatever God existed – they were going to know about it.

Having endured many separations from my parents during my early childhood and teen years, I was dreaming over and over again that I couldn't find my way home. I would be lost in strange cities, neighborhoods, trains, in the middle of the ocean, in elevators, always trying to find home. It was clear what those dreams meant since, in the past, I had no home in my shifting, unstable family. And until Amy became encased in armor and bullied her way through to work and financial success, there would be no home. That Amy created "home." But a predictable finale occurred during the critical stage of my illness – the armor blew up and off. My Statue became dust. There was no Amy; thus there was no home. I was brand spanking new and raw, raw, raw. Naked, I faced the future.

Blow the House Down

Then there was this intense railroad theme that kept emerging over and over again in my dreams. It was intriguing because train travel had been such a huge part of my life. Taking the train into New York City was a weekly adventure for my mother, Little Carla and me (and, sometimes, Howard) when I was young and could still be carefree at times. We dressed up in our "good" clothes to visit my Dad at work and go shopping. My sister and I would look out the window and, well before entering the Grand Central tunnel, use a monotone repetitive phrase as we categorized buildings as "all beat up" or "all brand new." To us children, it was a long ride and gave us plenty of time to play. I imagined that the emergency pull cord, if used, would quickly hang the driver, thus stop the train. My sister was the best audience for my humor.

Our mother always sat apart from us.

My mother, "Little Carla," me, and Howard (standing) in New York City; c1964.

We also made regular pilgrimages to visit our well-to-do cousins on the Upper East Side. These were my mother's cousins and their lives revolved around food. Once the mammoth breakfast was done, they would plan for lunch. No sooner was lunch picked over that dinner was the topic of conversation. A fussy eater, I was often mocked but still fed.

I hated going there because my mother's first cousin married a man who often made derogatory comments about my father in front of me and, in fact, once referred to me as "the bastard child." He was a rich, overweight angry man and I loathed our family visits other than visiting my blind Great Aunt Gisela who lived in their spare bedroom and my cousins who sometimes played with me. 'Auntie Gizzy' was kind and spent time with me, the two things my young life lacked. I recall the rope strung between her bed and the bathroom so she could feel her way there. I also remember how my sister and I laughed at the horrible, second-hand gifts they would give us like sweaters or scarves or chachkes that had no meaning.

Two other train trips bring happier memories. On one trip, the whole family (at that time included two intact parents, two half siblings – Little Carla and Howard – and me) traveled to Georgia for my father's business but also for pleasure. All I remember is the train and having such fun with my siblings in a cramped cabin as we whizzed by unfamiliar places. They slept in bunk beds while I remember sleeping on a teeny, tiny cot.

At age 14, I took a solo trip to Boston to visit Little Carla in college. The train was old-school with cloth and metal seats and, to my delight, broke down often. The seats folded back so six passengers could face each other and socialize; you could open all the windows and feel the breeze. There were three of us who bonded in our passenger compartment and the older conductor took a liking to me and let me stand between the cars while the train moved. I enjoyed the sights, sounds and his company.

In our little group, I met a thirty-something Vietnam War veteran who had lost several fingers but was drawing and sketching like a pro. He drew a picture of me that I have since lost. I also met a niece of Tom Carvel who couldn't have been more different than me – prep school pretty, matching luggage, and delightfully spoiled. She was at most 17, still in high school, and at least we had that in common. She took on the role of protector of me a bit on the six hour trip that should have taken four. I never wanted that train trip to end yet was still delighted when I saw my now-college age sister, Little Carla, waiting for me as I stepped off the train.

So going "home" by whatever means of travel was significant to me. Home also meant the sticks and bricks that Will, Daniel, Brett and I called "home." There was our little loving family there and caring neighbors surrounding it. At the time, home was a small ranch house, one bathroom, three bedrooms and a finished basement along with nice outdoor property and close, needed proximity to dear neighbors.

But somebody or something huffed and puffed and blew Amy away and settling in anywhere would prove difficult. During many nights back at "home," I woke leaping out of bed in panic, breathing hard and hiding in the corners or in the closets. I cried incessantly, sometimes from panic within and sometimes from actual pain. Real or imagined, I did not feel safe – anywhere. I continued to heal and receive excellent medical care even though every doctor I saw said my case was an "anomaly." Lupus plus cancer do not a good mix make. When my case went before the first hospital's Tumor Board, my doctors gloated and used my case as a horrible example of what can go wrong. My unbreakable husband embodied "for better or for worse, in sickness and in health." Although different, his ordeal from the outside looking in was horrific and I will never minimize what he experienced.

Often, I felt worse for him than I did for myself. We both went through the stages of grief once again (similar to when his dear nephew, Richie, died 10 years earlier) because even though now, no true death occurred, a trauma of this proportion impacted us like a meteor. We held each other close, cried, raged, and carried on post chemo.We had both read When Bad Things Happen to Good People by Rabbi Harold Kushner and, now, we read it again. And I read – carefully – Elizabeth Kubler Ross' book On Death and Dying. I slowly understood her descriptions of the five stages of grief as compared to our experiences now: 1) Denial and Isolation; 2) Anger; 3) Bargaining; 4) Depression; and 5) Acceptance.

I stumbled through each one of these steps for nearly three years to reach a "new normal." Throughout the years that have followed, I've continually had to check my cancer, battle chemotherapy side effects that kill certain aspects of my functioning that are immunologic, neurological, gastrointestinal, musculoskeletal and psychiatric, undergo numerous surgeries, endure broken bones, and Lupus flares. I have incorporated these five stages into my very nature as well as adapted to numerous "new normals."

From 1998 through 2000, little by little, my brain began to function again, but words spoken by others sounded garbled sometimes, like the adults in the Peanuts cartoons. 'Waw waw waw wah wah'. I couldn't feel water temperature with my fingers so I bought a little floating duck thermometer to make sure the boys' bathwater wouldn't scald them. For a long time, I turned completely inward, hiding my faults at normal functioning. Yet that is when I started to take back some control. It is also when the true personal education of the sum and total of my life to date began.

If the original Amy was to return (if I could find her), I had to take control. It started with a simple markdown on my closet door. I made a crude sign on poster paper that listed the numbers 18 down to 0. After each chemo treatment, I would cross off one with a dark, ugly marker. I was thrilled when 18 became 16 because I was able to cross off three at once. I had two daily "good thoughts" calendars and I would paste the ones I liked on that closet door. I kept a table next to the couch arranged with pictures of my boys, mail, books, drinks, meds and papers. If someone moved something even slightly out of place, I had to restore it, at once. The framed wallet-sized photograph of my children always went with me to the hospital.

I discovered music once again, some new and some old. Prior to the trauma, I had been an avid country music fan. For reasons unknown, I lost my taste for Country Western and I joked that it was like Archie Bunker who, in one episode, received a blood transfusion from an African-American neighbor and the politically incorrect punch line was that he would now like fried chicken and watermelon. I had so many transfusions, surely I would be changed biologically as well, I thought.

Next, I found myself returning to old childhood and teen favorites including folk and light rock – Peter, Paul and Mary, Carole King, James Taylor, John Denver, Anne Murray, Linda Rondstadt, Bette Midler ballads and even some early Madonna. I discovered a new spiritual singer – Enya and Marcy Music which is supposed to mimic sounds you might hear in heaven. I found Barbra Streisand's "On Higher Ground" that she penned and sang for President Bill Clinton's dying mother and I also learned of a Broadway singer named Laurie Beecham who recorded a final CD before dying of cancer.

When I could, I read; self-help books and healthy lifestyle books. I learned about more methods to cure or keep oneself free of cancer than I could follow. I didn't know where to turn or what to eat! I became ardently afraid of food and tried to imagine myself following a macrobiotic diet or the complicated, assured disease-free diet that Dr. Andrew Weil espoused in his books. In the following years, I did try

Getting lost in books was always my passion.

several methods and, finally, resumed my own healthful diet and lifestyle that I had followed for years with some changes because of what my body can accommodate and what it could not tolerate.

I drew. As a child, my mother had urged me to take drawing classes because I did have a natural talent. Alas, I didn't take those classes thus my drawing style was still crude but not bad. I drew a series of cartoons called "Chemo Kelly" and shared them with my infusion nurses. The cartoons helped encapsulate my experiences without speaking of them and revived a bit of the humor that had existed in the old Amy.

I did not write, although I did keep some sort of daily diary. When I was too ill, many entries would be missing but I was trying to record my experiences then, as a fake sort of Amy, not the Amy who would once again rise like a Phoenix and be in charge, in control, and encased in armor once again as my Statue stood tall. I still sought the real Amy desperately and with some craziness. Yes, of course, I believed I would return to her. Of course she would return to me. Of course, I was dead wrong; or was I?

Solitude, however forced, was all I had known for a very long period of time and I damn well needed it; time makes sense of the nonsensical. I asked myself many questions. What is spirit? Soul? Faith? What is life? Death? Was my Amy house simply a house of cards? Did I have enough chutzpah to pull this off; or, perhaps, enough naiveté? Or… should … I … just … let … go? It would be so much easier.

I did write my funeral arrangements and included the songs "Wind Beneath My Wings" for Will and "There Is A Balm in Gilead," a favorite hymn. I also wrote the words I wanted spoken aloud. I watched and listened for sights or sounds that would give me the answers. Often, all I could do, because of pain and discomfort, was to lie flat in bed, without television or music, and remain immobile while home life went on outside by bedroom door. As the spring rains came, I let the drops fall on my face through the window screen behind my bed. It was wonderful. I heard the first birdsongs and tried identifying them based on what my father had taught me.

One of the happier activities my Daddy and I shared when I was a child was walks-in-the-woods, inspecting the thousands of aspects of nature and identifying bird calls. I recalled Dad sitting in our broken down backyard in a lawn chair whistling to a bird only to find out the answering tweets came from our neighbor behind the fence. Now, if a solitary bird landed on the outside windowsill and chirped, peeped, or warbled at me, I decided it was a sign; my loving Daddy was near, not the one who went on vacation while I lay close to death.

I pictured myself as some sort of stone mason, rolling around in the muck trying to lay stones, trying, trying, trying to rebuild my Statue. It didn't work. Nothing seemed to work and my tears flowed unchecked. I seemed to cry for ages.

"I Hate Your Guts"

I was in remission.

"What," I said? "What's that?" I was so befuddled and befogged that I barely understood. "Really," I kept asking. "Really?" And it reminded me of how gullible I was as a 20-year-old newspaper reporter when the wicked, wizened news hands would tell me some wacky tale and I would say: "Really?" They would all laugh at my expense then and I thought it was funny, too. Now it was a miracle.

In my shattered state, I had new thoughts. Maybe I could beat this? Maybe I would live? Maybe the first small stone of my Statue had been re-laid; a toe, perhaps? Good enough for me. It would soon be time to rally, I thought. This wreck of a person was alive, barely, and now it was time to look forward.

Looking forward was all I could do. Some weeks later, at my first physical therapy session, they found that that even the simplest task, like stepping up a one-inch step, was difficult for me. I could hardly understand what they were saying, due to chemo brain, but I tried to follow their instructions. They were so kind. My physical therapist, remarked once that he hoped he wouldn't hear from me the four words he hated so much from patients. I croaked out: "I hate your guts?" He and his staff laughed. The four words they dreaded were: "You made me worse." In grueling and very small increments, I started to make physical progress. Gosh damn it; I think I even smiled once or twice as they tried to manipulate my weakened muscles into strength.

But this was the easy part: physical therapy, planning on the port removal, the neck reconstruction – all of which wouldn't be completed for a few years. For a short while, I was able to push the mental and spiritual aspects away. I would still wake up at night gasping for breath, eyes wide open in terror, sweating, crying, screaming. Would it ever end?

So there I was. Amy who? I had no clue. *Cancer survivor?* I refused to wear that label. *Working woman?* No longer applied. *Patient?* Forevermore. *Religious born-again?* No way. Yet, I was still a wife and mother and, during my initial recovery, I clung to that with fervor. I owed my husband and my kids. I had scared the hell out of them. I needed to make up for their prolonged fear. And make it up, I did.

I would get up and get the kids to school and then sleep or go to medical appointments until it was time for them to come home. I mustered up the energy to dress, apply makeup and be their joyful Mom; the Mom who now was trying to see the world in a positive way.

"Make a good day," I would chirp as they would leave for school in the morning until they both told me they hated that phrase. We did art projects, read books, watched movies; anything that would allow me to be seated yet involved and engaged.

Summer soon arrived and off we went to the pool. I would smile my crooked smile, peer hazily through my permanently weakened eyes, and disregard my peach fuzz hair as I led my kids to water. While they splashed and played with friends, I would pop pills and sleep under the umbrella. When folks would say how happy they were to see me, I would smile and say "thank you," wishing the hushed talk about my appearance, my ordeal, and my very survival wouldn't continue nearby.

I baked cookies, made fresh lunches and dinner and set the table with flair. I created fanciful birthday parties for the children and I danced the happy dance, clumsily and slowly. My husband and children responded. I had never worn the $450 full wig that we bought but I thought the wrap-around partial hair that attached with Velcro was hysterical. It needed a hat or scarf on top so I dressed up in it often to make the kids laugh, especially when I donned a crafted "Good Burger" hat after the popular 1997 kids' movie at the time and looked exactly like one of its characters.

Daniel, especially, was thrilled. His Mommy was back and could go to school functions without wearing a face mask and hospital bracelets. I could take him out for Halloween and make his costume again. He showered me with extra special love, drawing cards, writing poems and still smiling, laughing his hearty laugh. He has a wicked sense of humor and I would laugh from deep within and without cares or thoughts in the world. My work was over, career wrecked. With my dual diagnoses, I was immediately put on disability so when I was with Daniel, Brett, or Will I was WITH them.

Brett went on as always, gleeful even while in the throes of separation from his biological family and in the process of permanently joining ours. The actual adoption happened fast and we celebrated with special joy. I was there to witness it. My blurred eyes saw with clarity the amazing feat we had accomplished in adopting Brett. Once again, we were a family and the joy this little fellow brought into our lives was more than remarkable. His need made us better people. He continued to inspire and enlighten with his spirit, fortitude and generosity of love.

Adoption day. September 2000.

Like the pros after winning the Superbowl, We went to Disneyland. It was extremely difficult for me but I stumbled my way through, watched my husband and sons enjoy the rides and half slept, dizzy and nauseous, in Disney cafes while they waited in lines. The cafeteria with the costumed Bullwinkle, Boris and Natasha wafting around struck me as especially creepy as I thought I was hallucinating again. I put one foot in front of the other.

At Disney 1999.

We had a tradition at Christmas in which the boys would do their gift shopping at a local dollar store so they could choose and wrap a gift for everyone in our nuclear and extended families. That year, Daniel bought me a $1 shrink-wrapped set of "pearl and diamond" earrings and necklace. His pride in presenting them to me was palpable and I wore them the following week to a New Year's Eve party in my still-bloated from steroids body and very short hair. The earrings hurt terribly but they remain, to this day, in a special place in my jewelry box.

New Year's Eve with painful bloating (and earrings) 1998.

I felt eager to thank everyone who had helped me along the way. I presented many with friendship gifts and angel pins and it made me glad. I also started making friends – GIRL friends, to my own astonishment. I quickly discarded support groups as I found most participants would die, but I put myself out there for the first time, in this awful physical state, and introduced myself to the mothers of Daniel and Brett's friends. I would always start with, "You are meeting me at a very strange time in my life" and explain my recovery status, but some gems emerged. I think I made my first true woman friends during this time. I was open and my past work, most often with men, was no longer in my frontal lobe.

Also during this unusually aware period when every sense seemed to be seeing, hearing, tasting, smelling and feeling with a special acuteness, I recall two events with my children; one for its humor, the other for its snap-back to reality. Walter's, the famous hot dog stand in Mamaroneck, New York, is a seasonal place since it offers window service only. Our family would make regular treks to Walter's. The Walter's difference lies in its 100-years plus seasoned grill and how they use a secret buttery mixture to grill both the dogs and the buns. They are simply the best hot dogs in the world, attested to not only by locals but celebrities and politicos from every far flung spot imaginable. Postcards, dating as far back as the 1900s, adorn the structure,

In our little home, when I would grill hot dogs and rolls in butter, they became known as "Walter's hot dogs." Also in our home, were two Little Tykes weeble-wobble characters that came with Daniel's first toy fire truck. I don't know why, but when a very young Daniel asked me their names one day, I immediately blurted out Walter and Henry. The names stuck. Daniel and Brett played endlessly with Walter and Henry, both with and without their fire truck.

Cooking hot dogs one day, I called downstairs to the then nine-year-old Daniel and five-year-old Brett and told them what I was doing and I asked: "Do you want a Walter's?" This meant split and grilled with butter, of course. If they said "no," it meant whole and microwaved or boiled. Without hesitation, Daniel called back: "I'll have a Walter's!" And, a mere second later, I heard Brett, in his little voice call back: "I'll have a Henry!" We roared with laughter!!! As I write this, Walter and Henry sit right on my windowsill, long forgotten by the boys. I will never forget and just looking at them makes me recall one of the funniest, simplest moments of life with my children.

The second event jarred me back to reality. I had been overcompensating, of course, for being ill for so long and was up at about 7 a.m. making homemade pancakes for the crew. As I stood in the kitchen, spatula in hand, Daniel, who had already been up watching cartoons, walked in and proclaimed: "I wish we could be like a normal family and I could smell the pancakes cooking and that would wake me up." I stood there stunned. What the hell was I doing? Later, Daniel's query became legend and when the story is told, I always comment how it took me everything I had not to smack him hard with that spatula right then and there. Never anger a woman with spatula in hand!!! But, of course, it wasn't his fault. It was mine. I was creating monsters in need.

Denying myself wasn't smart, and my focus changed ever so slightly. I allowed myself some guilt-free healing time and a re-focus on how to achieve long-term health, work, and home balance, not just this short burst of Donna Reed. Again, my family had to adjust, and so they did.

It was especially important for me to thank the congregation at my Church and I did so in a speech. Those who were there that day watched me inch up the steps, wearing new glasses since my eyes had faded fast during treatment. Here is what I said to the good people of Briarcliff Congregational Church, Briarcliff Manor, New York:

Eight years ago, I nervously started attending this Church and sat among you wondering when I, a person who had no religious education whatsoever, would begin to feel the depth of what all of you seemed to be feeling. Oh, I got the routine down, learned and started speaking words I had never said before, stood when I should be standing and sat when I should be sitting, and started recognizing hymns as they would come up time and time again.

But in the deepest moments of prayer, I would ask God when I would see some kind of sign that this was right for me – that I should join the Church fully and wholly – be baptized among friends. Well, boy God, I got a heckuva sign!

As many of you know, this past year I have been gravely ill and have experienced things both medical and emotional that I never thought I could endure. But it was the palpable energy that emanated from here, from this very room, that finally gave me the gift of the spiritual. Because of that, I was baptized last Palm Sunday.

The energy of this Church, this congregation, without a doubt reached me. From the very beginning when I learned I would be undergoing difficult surgery, there was Joanne Picket*, nurse, right by my side with words of encouragement for both me and my family, even when the news was bad.

Then without warning, I experienced a life-threatening emergency and awoke to find Andrea Paulson*, nurse, at my side. Because of my condition, she couldn't recognize me and I couldn't speak, but I could write and when I told her who I was, I felt safe. Then again, nights later in ICU, a nurse appeared at my side. It was Karen LaGrange* who many of you may remember was a secretary here at this Church when I first joined. Coincidences? I don't think so.

And, of course, there was always Pastor Joseph* -- at each hospital, at each emergency throughout the year imparting his wisdom and support and teaching me how to pray. I have no doubt that the healing energy generated from your ongoing prayers, cards, gifts, visits, calls, and meals delivered to my home helped keep me aloft – were added fuel in my empty engine, so to speak – literally keeping me alive when I no longer had the strength to do it myself.

In October, my family and I gave a small gift to this Church. With help from the Buildings and Grounds Committee, we purchased and planted 500 crocus bulbs around the two Church signs. During one of my seemingly interminable hospital stays (where your mind has too much time to think), all I could think of was thanking all of you, which was a good thing and an important thing for me to do. And I decided the best way I could do that was to find some symbol of the life you were giving me and I chose crocuses, the first flowers of spring. It is a very small gesture that I hope you will all accept as a deeply heartfelt 'thank you' for all that you have done. I know when I drive by next spring and see them flowering, I will smile and think of all of you and the wondrous things that are accomplished here. It is my sincere wish that you will do the same, year after year.

Finally, also having plenty of time to read this past year, I came across a noteworthy statement penned by Dr. Elisabeth Kubler-Ross who writes on death and dying. It is a particularly appropriate quote to summarize my feelings here:

"I have never met a person whose greatest need was anything other than real, unconditional love. You can find it in a simple act of kindness toward someone who needs help. There is no mistaking love. You feel it in your heart. It is the common fiber of life, the flame that heats our soul, energizes our spirit and supplies passion to our lives. It is our connection to God and to each other."[5]

Along with my husband, Will, who exemplifies the meaning of for better or for worse, in sickness and in health; my son, Daniel, who has shown depths of compassion and strength I didn't know could exist in a seven-year-old boy; my foster son, Brett, who will be our blessing during 1998 when it

---

[5] On Death and Dying; Elisabeth Kubler Ross; Scribner; 1St Edition (June 9, 1997)

appears we will be able to have him permanently join our family even though he's already indelibly marked our hearts; I thank you and God bless you all.

The crocuses in bloom.

I received a tearful standing ovation and at last realized, finally, that my life had been changed forever – changed, once and for all, for the good. The silver lining was perceptible.

The Towers Fall and Daddy Dies

Still living with daily fear, however, I found extreme rage towards the doctor who had missed my diagnosis. He was an easy target. One day, when I was at the hospital to get a Nupigen shot, a white cell enhancer, I called him down to the emergency room. The ER was quite empty and I heard Dr. C being paged. Allied with the station nurse, we called him down, an ambush so to speak. Face-to-face now, I confronted him.

"Look what you did to me," I cried. "Just look!" I showed him the scars, the hole in my neck that had healed and twisted my neck and trachea into an unspeakable knot, the horror of my appearance. He apologized and said he "made a muh…" He never finished the word mistake. He asked to still be involved in my care. I told him to get the hell out.

It was a hollow victory so I brought a malpractice lawsuit by finding a reputable New York City law firm that specialized in women's health issues. They took my case on contingency. It wasn't until three years later I learned it was contingent upon my death. One of the hugest smacks in the face I ever took was when the lawyer pulled me out of the deposition room and said: "You have no case. You lived. We only take these cases knowing you will die." For many months I had to restrain myself from driving my mini-van through the hated doctor's office or enacting some other heinous crime against him. At last, I decided, he had to live with his own hell. I was done with him. That was my victory.

I forged through many setbacks during the next five years, biopsy surgeries for new hot spots and the live and in living color neck reconstruction. My first ever mammogram revealed an area of concern and, boom, back in the operating room again. It wasn't cancer; it was something called a radial scar. I had the port removed and began treatments for Lupus and the many ongoing side effects from the chemo. Growing like weeds they are now severe osteoporosis, corrosive esophagitis, balance and vertigo issues, gastroparesis, confusion, incomprehension, lack of a body temperature gauge, headaches, nausea from medication, difficulty swallowing and talking, drastic eyesight change, depression and anxiety. Also, I have the interminable terror of IT returning. Fear is, I think, my middle name. Fear comes and goes but mostly, stays around. Learning how to loosen its grip on me is, I think, the hugest challenge of all.

My relationships with my parents changed. It sounds self-centered unless you know my family history, that I gave them back the gift of me. I visited and worked hard at getting to know them as people rather than parents. I learned much about what drove their early lives and the lives they had chosen now. There were no revelations, per se, but there was a tacit reconciliation. Many years later, as they each suffered prolonged deaths (my father in 2002 and my mother in 2008), I was the one who sat by their sides and took care of their needs. I needed to do it for myself and I am forever grateful for that time I had with them.

Admitted to a nursing home just two blocks away from me, my father had six months to live. I visited daily, bringing him home-cooked meals, recounting current family stories and showing him the latest PowerPoint work I was doing on my computer. My children and husband also visited, as we could all walk, bike or rollerblade there. The nursing home staff and residents accepted us, even as Dan and Brett skated through the halls, or when Brett snuggled up to my father and fell asleep for a long nap. I was able to leave and come back when he woke up.

On September 11, 2001, my Bronx-based firefighter husband received the urgent summons to New York City after the first plane hit the Twin Towers. I hustled to my children's schools and brought them home; then I ran to the nursing home, bursting in to make a beeline for my father's private room. He wasn't there.

As I looked around the television room, I found him – blending in with the other patients. Daddy matched the collective breath-taking horror that was unfolding on the big screen TV. There I stood, in front of the half-dozing patients, the wife of a firefighter somewhere amid the inexplicable crumple of the Twin Towers and the daughter of a man who looked exactly like his peers as he died very slowly.

I sat down and sobbed, listening to the whistles and beeps of the patients' various life-giving machines along with the loud, bird-like chirps emanating from the TV screen – the tweets from the alert units within each firefighter's uniform that indicated "firefighter down." The firefighters were buried under the gray ash; the nursing home patients awash in their own illness and/or drug-induced daze. It was a symphony of grief.

My father always wanted to get out of the nursing home but was popular among its patients and staff. Borrowing a neighbor's portable wheelchair, I went up and "sprung" him, half-walking but being forced to run down my non-side walked street's steep decline amid the fallen leaves and bumping purposely into a lawn now and then so I wouldn't lose my grip. My father was laughing and smiling and breathless with glee.

Making the sharp turn into my own driveway, I steered the wheelchair into my back yard, navigated another grassy slope down through sliding glass doors into our finished basement. Opening a sofa bed, I helped ease him out of the wheelchair, deposited him in the bed with pillows and blankets and then I slumped into a chair – exhausted. He smiled and took a nap.

My husband reappeared after yet another tour of recovery duty in "the pile" at the World Trade Center site and he helped my father into the small wheelchair and rolled him back up the steep hill, into his room and bed. I had to take a nap.

I reflected on how far we had come as father and daughter; I was now mothering him and he yielded his stubborn streak to allow it. My father was a conundrum. His gaiety, sparkling eyes, love of life, intelligence, humor and charm resurfaced in his small and shriveled body and we enjoyed some laughs and serious talks. Over and over again, he said, "I love you." And I would reply: "I know Dad. I love you, too." The years of pain seemed to melt away as we said these final goodbyes over six short months.

The night before my father died was extraordinary. It was January 8th, 2002 and Brett and I were visiting him. He could no longer speak yet his eyes remained fixed on my every move. When he grasped my hand, I understood what the "death grip" meant. He was breathing rapidly. I asked him if he was in any pain. He shook his head, 'no.' I asked him if he wanted something to drink. He shook his head, 'no.' I had to go to the bathroom; I peeled back each of his fingers with great difficulty and somehow transferred his hand from mine to Brett's. His head turned with my movements, his eyes floating along while I walked to the bathroom in his room while Brett said: "Ouch. He's strong." And I said: "Yes. He always was."

After I returned and reclaimed his clasping hand and his steady, unblinking gaze, he dozed off finally closing his eyes. Brett and I watched the rise and fall of his chest and listened to his shallow but steady breathing to make sure he was asleep. His grip loosened and Brett and I went home. I knew he would die that night at age 82.

The next day at 9 a.m., I received the phone call that he had, indeed, passed. I went to see his body. I cried and made the required phone calls to my brother, Steve, and sister, Big Carla, and left before the funeral home arrived. It was a peaceful reconciliation and passing; however I wore one of his sweaters for a year – its smell and scratchy wool gave me comfort.

My mother's nursing home experiences were vastly different. One evening in 2003, I was summoned to her new senior citizen studio apartment. The apartment was situated geographically in-between Little Carla's house and mine in order that we could help with her

138

chores and visit her. On this evening by phone, my mother told me, breathlessly, that she was having a heart attack. I said, "No, you're not" and drove on over slowly. I proceeded to witness, what I was certain, was an anxiety attack since she hated this new apartment and wanted company seven days a week, 24 hours a day. She said, "No. I can't breathe," something I'd heard and seen many times before.

Without giving her credence, I called 911 and the ambulance and its attendants arrived. Dumping her numerous over-prescribed psychiatric medicines out of a drawer into a plastic bag, I said I would follow them to the hospital but that it was no emergency; she was simply having a panic attack. I watched her get loaded into the ambulance from my own car's driver seat and pulled out slowly, traveling behind the ambulance without sirens the six miles to the nearest community hospital. I even grabbed some of her magazines so I would have something to read in the waiting room.

About a half hour later, a doctor swung open the "Do Not Enter" door and peered into the waiting room. He asked: "Who is with Mrs. Crohn?" I got up slowly and indicated it was me. He took me just into the doorway and said: "Your mother's very ill. She's had a serious heart attack." Astonished, I said: "Really?" (I was back in the newsroom again.) He assured me it was so and I was dumbfounded. The lady who cried wolf so often finally had suffered the real thing!

I then found it necessary to call my brother, Howard, and my sister, Little Carla, to inform them of the news. The next few days in the hospital were a blur but my mother was informed that she needed major heart surgery or would live only six months. She refused the surgery. She was told to go home to her senior apartment and she would be eligible for an upgrade to a two-bedroom and a live-in aide. She refused that, too. The only thing I could get her to accept was an assisted living facility. Over the next six years (yes, she lived six more years without the surgery), she moved from one facility to another, burning bridges at each one by being cruel to staff or making up bold–faced lies ("They're banging my head against the wall!).

The stress on Little Carla, my husband, Will, and I were immeasurable. Howard helped, too, but the act of physically moving her things each time she refused to return to an assisted living or nursing facility after a hospital stay, was largely left to Will, Little Carla and me. With each move, we culled more of her stuff, finally putting most of it in a storage facility. At the end of this three-years-long ordeal, she landed, like a deflated balloon, at her final resting place – a nursing home two miles away from my house.

I tried dutifully to visit her as I had with my Dad but it was not the same. Her anger, sadness, and madness were intolerable. As the doctors prescribed her stronger and stronger "cocktails" of psychotropic drugs, she finally became calm, yet her spirit had been subdued. She no longer seemed to be herself. I felt pity and overwhelming sadness.

One of my most vivid memories during this time is of pushing her in a wheelchair (unlike my father who couldn't walk anymore, my mother refused to walk) and I asked: "Mom. You know what you're like?" I don't even recall what my answer was going to be but her answer struck me hard, like a slap. "A Black Widow spider," she said, "because I eat my young." Aha! I knew she was a spider all along.

And so it was an apt ending to my story with my mother. She died on December 31, 2008 at age 85, a protracted death; uncomfortable except for the medications that kept her immobile and drugged into a near coma. I mourned deeply but quickly. I am truly happy she is finally at peace.

The Science

Today, I am healing again from a painful fall a few days ago on a walk with friends where I lost my balance and crashed to the pavement. I twisted my ankle and cut and bruised my knee, elbow and wrist. I also just finished a series of tests (including a 24–hour tube down my nose and into my throat) to figure out how to improve my swallowing, the persistent lump in my throat, and raspiness; and I have scheduled a follow-up endoscopy to see if the stage four lesions on my esophagus have healed after three years of treatment. I hold a prescription for a CT scan with contrast for so-far-unidentifiable chest pain which could indicate a tumor return. I continue to allot my weekly medicines into daily containers. It makes me recall my first oncologist saying: "You are with me for life." And, in my naiveté, I looked at her thinking 'that will never happen.' When I am done with cancer, I am done. The reality, I continue to learn a dozen or so years later, is that nothing is further from the truth.

I did try to go back to work, full-time, as a marketing director. It was my trial work period from disability. My resumed career lasted nearly three years although I had two biopsy surgeries and broken bones that got in the way. It was a challenging and fun three years, however. I was glad I gave it all I had and made new friends. We laughed uproariously one day when I realized I had popped two Tic-Tacs in my mouth (for minty fresh breath to take away the taste from all the medications I was prescribed) and washed them down with water before I realized they weren't a dose of my pills.

Thereafter, I resumed my relationship with the medical community and now I regard one of my daily jobs as monitoring and caring for my health. When I get fed up with the tests, the medicines, anything that even remotely has a caduceus symbol, I take a break. But I know if I skip my medicines for just one week, I will be back in the hospital – a place that I have both run to and run away from in delirium. One surgery was postponed because I took out my own IV and ran out of the operating bay with flashbacks to an earlier time. It never gets easier.

I often think about the state of medical care in the United States, especially with drastic health care reform debates underway. However, a few troubling thoughts always bubble to the surface. Scientists develop medicines that prolong lives. With the right medications in some cases, even cancer can be considered a chronic illness. So we live longer, perhaps better and enjoy more years; but at what expense to us as individuals? To our families? To our nation? What is one life worth? And is one life worth more than another to receive extended treatment? I know these very questions weigh heavily among the medical community, health insurance professionals, lobbyists, and politicians. I know they weigh heavily on me.

Dr. Akoury sums it up this way: "You cannot be wealthy unless you are healthy. Kind of like the chicken and the egg, which comes first? If you have enough wealth to buy the best in healthcare, would that make you healthy? Wealth may give you better odds, but you can't buy health. It takes much more than expensive prescription medications and countless visits to the doctor to create a healthy environment within your body."

Every day, I take more than a half-dozen different medications. Some of these drugs did not exist two years ago. As I review the symptoms of the chronic diseases and disorders I battle and review them side-by-side with the side effects of my many medicines, I become confused. What am I doing? Am I helping or hurting myself by being so smart and efficient by taking such good care of myself? Again, I question: 'Should…I….just….let….go?" Long ago promised by many different doctors that they would be "captains of my ship" to help manage questions like this, none delivered. I stay adrift, wrestling with my health and care, knowing that, other than God, I am the only one that can be in any kind of control today – my own chief executive officer, as Dr. Akoury says. Perhaps integrative medicine is in my future. In fact, I know it is.

About a year after my father's death in 2002, I opened the last container of his belongings and found voluminous carbon copies of letters to his lawyer during my parents' divorce and my mother's subsequent appeals to court for more money. As I read and read and read, I noted that references to me began as his "treasured little girl" and ended as "The Amy Problem," as he referred to me and my needs as a growing teen. The timing was right because if I had read any of this in years prior, I don't think I could have thrown it all away when I finished. Our history was over; done. In the end, I knew where his heart lay after our relationship healed through his bonding with my sons and his help in nursing me back to health.

I've done some free-lance consulting work and I've babysat. I took care of my dying parents and I extend myself to friends, acquaintances and strangers whenever I can. I helped my grown up Dan with his college search and applications and my high schooler, Brett, with his homework and scheduling. Both my boys are fully engaged with school, sports and work. I cook, clean and do laundry. I spend romantic and quiet times with my husband and crazy times with my friends. Some days, if I overextend, I stay in bed the next.

Rarely, I let others peek behind my iron curtain and reveal certain details of my pained childhood, life's path, sickness and, even, death. It is then that I hear the questioning exhortation over and over again: "But, you look so good?" I never know whether or not the question is meant as a compliment but I choose to take it as such. I want to talk to tell them that I am simply the protagonist in one of my favorite children's books balancing ten apples on top of his head. The talented tiger in <u>Ten Apples Up On Top</u> by Dr. Seuss shows his skill in this readily available manner. As a sickly adult, I envision myself balancing those apples – but my balance is far more precarious. The apples and I can fall.

When my balance was still good. 1971.

I still check in with my Statue because it remains the only constant that is accurate. It is my inner visibility; my daily time clock. Today, my Statue stands tall with a slight crack in its knee cap and an ankle turned sideways. That's how I fell and that's where it hurts. I always acknowledge my Statue and its mysterious truth.

In fact, I later learned childhood maltreatment is linked to increased risk of adult disease with inflammatory origin. In recent studies that are seeking to alleviate serious adult illness by recognizing and then interrupting this childhood pattern, researchers in Australia and New Zealand proved that their study group patients who were maltreated as children were 95 per cent more likely to be in poor health as adults and experience adult physical illness of an inflammatory nature.

According to one of the lead researchers, *"around one in 10 children worldwide is exposed to maltreatment including psychological, physical or sexual abuse, or neglect and as a result abnormalities can show up in biological areas that are particularly sensitive to stress, such as the brain and the immune system."*

Hmmmm. The immune system?

The researchers suggest that good health "is not a state but a lifetime achievement." Moreover, they say, understanding the childhood developmental processes and mechanisms that "get under the skin" leave enduring health signatures. I find this research to be uncannily spot on in my case.[6]

Furthermore, a separate 2009 study reveals: *"Babies whose mothers are attentive and caring tend to grow into happy, well-adjusted children. But the psychological benefits of having a doting mother may extend well beyond childhood."*[7]

A doting mother?

Yet another research study that surveyed more than 17,000 adults was the beginning of a decades-long collaboration between the Federal Centers of Disease Control and Prevention and Kaiser Permanente. Called the Adverse Childhood Experiences (ACE) study, the results established a clear connection between harmful childhood experiences and later negative health effects. Participants were given a numeric grade based on childhood exposure to sub-categories of abuse, neglect, and household dysfunction. Astonishingly, my childhood experience correlates to most of the sub-categories.[8]

Finally, yet another researcher and expert, Ellen Taliaferro, MD, FACEP, Medical Director, Keller Center for Family Violence Intervention; San Mateo Medical Center, San Mateo, California and Director, Health After Trauma Project – Addressing the Medical

---

[6] Andrea Danese, Carmine M. Pariante, Avshalom Caspi, Alan Taylor, and Richie Poulton; Proceedings of the National Academy of Sciences of the United States of America (PNAS), January 23, 2007; © 2007 by The National Academy of Sciences of the USA

[7] Joanna Maselko, Ph.D., Duke University Medical School, in Durham, North Carolina

[8] Robert Anda, M.D. and Vincent Felitti, M.D., California Institute of Preventive Medicine; The Adverse Childhood Effects (ACE) Study is ongoing collaborative research between the Centers for Disease Control and Prevention in Atlanta, GA, and Kaiser Permanente in San Diego, CA

Effects of Trauma and Abuse; Creekside Communications. Reno, Nevada, comments:

"The ACE Study researchers recommend an approach that addresses the early childhood trauma as well as the adult disease and distress. When treating patients with past adverse childhood events, these physicians augment standard pharmacological treatment with the use of medical interviews and autobiographical writing to explore how their patients perceive that the earlier childhood events have shaped their adult life and well-being."

All of the researchers and doctors recommend treating adult onset disease with an eye toward investigating childhood maltreatment, including patient interviews, journaling, and extensive medical and personal histories.

So how does this all relate to me; my case? Could I really use my abnormal childhood as a direct link to Lupus and cancer; to this horrible, terrible, near-fatal crescendo? I ponder these results and find that, if I wanted to, I could tie all of my life's experiences into a nice neat bow and 'blame' my parents if I accepted these studies and research without question. But they do give me pause – to reflect and think and listen carefully to those who are expert in mind-body connection. My Statue has become The Thinker, the bronze and marble sculpture by Auguste Rodin.

If, in truth, the reason my tumor was centered in my heart was because my heart was so cut off from unconditional love that it put layers upon layers upon layers of armor on itself for protection, perhaps it was my time to implode. The fact that I was, as a married adult, very emotionally disconnected from those other than my own, little nuclear family, I realized I feared emotional connection like others fear a broken nail or bad haircut. But now, when I found myself hyperventilating in my closet, I knew I had to make a choice between using many coats of spackle to become closed again or learning how to remain open.

I did not want to blame or become the victim forevermore. So, I consciously chose the latter and have spent many years practicing its creed. It was a relief to finally feel that armor blown away, through no conscious effort of my own. The insight helped me, and "the truth shall set you free." My body finally untied some of the knots in my neck, shoulders, stomach and chest. With some bewilderment, I am still here with a healed heart both literally and figuratively.

And I am the one who reminds myself to always find the funny; the everyday humor in even the most mundane things – like the man who tried to leave his shopping cart askance in the grocery store lot and, as he drove off, the cart rolled clear across to hit a Mercedes SUV whose owner purposely parked in two spots to avoid his car being dented.

I'm the unarmored, strange lady who sidles up to waiting patients on hospital gurneys and in wheel chairs abandoned in the hallways to strike up a gentle conversation. "How are you today?" I ask. I'll pat their hand; give them thumbs up. Anything to let them know I know how they feel.

It's me, envisioning my Statue, as I listen to friends or family relate horror stories of illness and make split second decisions on whether I can stay and listen or bolt. I revel in my good days and languish on the bad. And I still fight hard with doctors and nurses when I disagree with their treatment of me.

Most of all, I am you – despondent over the ills of the world at large and triumphant over life measured in seconds at home.

EPILOGUE

It is with much relief that I find I am still among the living even with the many ailments I must manage. And it is with great grief that I have witnessed friends and families lose their medical battles, particularly with cancer, and I have to ask: "Why me?" Why am I still here? Why was I spared?

To me, the answer is this book and how it can ease others' anguish; empower the ill to challenge their doctors; change the course of medical treatment by lifting a veil and inspiring more research; creating a path toward true integrative medicine that will prove to be of most benefit to all of us who seek to live long, rich lives. In fact, I have volunteered to immerse myself in integrative/functional medicine as a 'guinea pig' of sorts to see how the final third of my life can be managed differently; perhaps with more comfort and less reliance on pharmaceuticals with so many side effects.

Our 'new normal.' In Cape May, New Jersey. 2000

I live my life in hopeful increments mostly centered on my children - graduation from high school, college, careers, marriage, grandchildren and my husband and I retiring to our beautiful condominium in South Carolina. I will still write, however, to share my new experiences and help others along with myself live a daring, fulfilling life. And I still have goals. Next up: I am going to be trained to become a Court Appointed Special Advocate for children in the foster care system. Children who are in difficult situations always need a separate voice. I don't want them to get sick as adults.

Lastly, I return to the very wise bear Pooh who says:

"Things just happen in the right way, at the right time. At least when you let them, when you work with circumstances instead of saying, 'This isn't supposed to be happening this way,' and trying harder to make it happen some other way."

Benjamin Hoff; The Tao of Pooh

ACKNOWLEDGEMENTS

I would be remiss if I did not acknowledge those who have supported me through my physical and emotional crises as well as lent a hand, an ear, a meal or slept on our couch, etc. through my numerous surgeries and hospitalizations to date.

First and foremost, I thank my husband, Will, and my sons, Daniel and Brett for their unwavering love for me as I spent so much time away from them recovering from one hospitalization or another plus the writing of this book. My siblings – Carla Crohn Friedman, Stephen Lyon Crohn, Howard Heller, and Carla Crohn Pellicci have been marvelously patient, loving and agreeable as I wrote of things that, perhaps, they didn't want shared but understood my need to heal. My extended family: Gina Pellicci, Amanda Shechter, Leslie Rosenberg, Todd Friedman, their spouses and 11 total children whom I love dearly and have been blessed to watch grow from birth to adulthood.

While now departed, I honor the memory and support of my parents, Richard and Norma Crohn, my nephews Richard Louis Venturo and John Stephen Venturo, and my brother-in-law, Vincent Charles Santagata. I will miss you and treasure our memories forever.

I must acknowledge my outstanding neighbors who became family to us all: Barbara and Frank Vassallo and their daughters, Dawn and Francine; and Fran and Nick Caldarola. Also, the staff of Happy Tots Day Care Center in Croton-on-Hudson, New York, who took care of my boys when I was not able and my husband had to go to work.

I learned prayer and patience from Pastors George Higgins, David Powers, and Bonnie Rosborough of Briarcliff Congregational Church, Briarclif Manor, New York. Thank you, too, to all the parishioners at this wonderfully soulful place.

Writer and friend Laura Shaine Cunningham, has gone above and beyond to enable me to transform my story into a feasible memoir. She was always available to answer my questions, offer advice and banter back and forth as I sought to make sense of the nonsensical, at times.

I thank all my fantastic friends and work colleagues – past and present – because friendships last for a "reason or a season or a lifetime." I am indebted to you all. Special thanks to Shelley Lynworth, Carol Oppenheimer, and Dr. Arthur Fass for reading a final draft and offering their comments and to Sherry Vance for her tireless efforts in getting all the photographs 'just right.'

Finally, although my relationships with medical doctors are sometimes precarious, there are those gems that remain in my heart and my soul forevermore. Their care was superlative in the face of terrible odds. I am forever grateful to medical doctors Arthur Fass, Franklin Zimmerman, Tauseff Ahmed, Nancy Mills, Abraham Mittleman, Robert Raniolo, Rocco LaFaro, David Lans, Richard Findling, Michael Lockshin, and Barry Jaffin. Thanks to the following mental health doctors and practitioners for putting my head back on straight: Ronald Rosen, Maurice Markevich, and Cassandra Roth. And for keeping me physically upright, I must thank chiropractors Scott Barry and Richard Finewood along with the physical therapy staffs at Club Fit, Briarcliff Manor, New York and Phelps Memorial Hospital, Sleepy Hollow, New York.

Thank you to all the dear attending nurses and technicians at Phelps Memorial Hospital, Sloan Kettering Cancer Center in Westchester and New York City; Westchester Medical Center, Valhalla, New York; White Plains Hospital, White Plains, New York; and Northern Westchester Hospital, Mount Kisco, New York. Some of them saw me time and time again.

Last but not least coming to my aid whenever I had a question or needed a research source or a physician referral was David Sachar, M.D., Board of Directors, Burrill B. Crohn Research Foundation, New York, New York.

To those I have neglected to mention, you know who you are and I apologize for the omission. I am forever indebted to you for your kindness and care during the most difficult times of my life.

AUTHOR BIOGRAPHY

Amy Susan Crohn is an accomplished marketing communications, business development professional, writer and journalist. She began her career in 1980 as a newspaper reporter at The Ocean County Times Observer, Toms River, N.J.

Thereafter, she worked for the American Heart Association, Rye, N.Y. as public relations and special events coordinator and for Time, Inc. as an editor at a start-up magazine, TV-Cable Week. She continued at American Water Works Company, Inc. (NYSE: AWK) in Greenwich, CT as director of community relations.

After leaving American Water Works in 1989, Amy started her own company becoming expert in water utility communications throughout the United States. During the 10 years she was in that business, she directed multiple corporate communications projects including research, creative copy writing, budgeting, project control, artistic direction and overall project production, serving international clientele in a variety of industries, including notable corporations such as AT&T, IBM, and PepsiCo. She is a skilled public speaker.

Amy also developed an interactive Executive Media Workshop to teach high-level managers and corporate CEOs how to manage the media spotlight. She was invited to present this workshop at a number of companies and associations across the tri-state area. Amy also taught a Public Relations course at Mercy College, White Plains, N.Y. for two years as an adjunct.

Since 2003, she has worked on copy writing, consulting and/or marketing projects for numerous private clients. She also works on her own writing projects that include both fiction and non-fiction works.

APPENDICES

APPENDIX A: S/Sgt Crohn – "MEMOIRS"

(AUTHOR'S NOTE: This is a re-formatted transcription of the following documents including errors in spelling and punctuation.)

An abridgement of the travels of the 114th Medical Battalion Clearing Company in combat from 7 September 1944 to VE Day, the 8th of May, 1945.

STATION: Videscosville, (France)

DATE: 7 Sept 44

MILES: 19

REMARKS: Arrived Cherbourg France at 10:00 (France) A.M. Disembarked at 1130 Traveled   by truck 15 miles to sorting point. Hiked a LONG 4 miles – in the rain – to bivouac area in Videscosville. "A Salute to Videscosville, whose motto is: 'Hines Cleared to Hedges'"!

STATION: Videscosville

DATE: 15 Sept 44

MILES:

REMARKS: 10 of our truck drivers trfd to 263rd FA Bn to serve as drivers on the "Red Ball Highway." Daily class in French.

STATION: Carteret (Les Moitiers d'Allonne)

DATE: 27 Sept 44

MILES: 27-46

REMARKS: Station established in tents in field overlooking bay. Boys have first sample of the Normandy Special: Calvedos and ofdre! Rumers: Elements of YD committed on 3rd Army front.

STATION: Le Mans

DATE: 18 Oct 44

MILES: 172-218

REMARKS: Left Carteret bivouac area at 0815. Traveled 172 miles to vicinity of Le Mans.

STATION: Lonjumeau

DATE: 19 Oct 44

MILES: 120-388

REMARKS: Left Le Mans 0920. Traveled 120 miles, and bivouacked on a famed race track near Paris.

STATION: Revigny

DATE: 20 Oct 44

MILES: 162-500

REMARKS: Left Lonjumeau at 0830. Bartered for ofdre along the way.

STATION: Cercueil (Vicinity of Nancy)

DATE: 21 Oct 44

MILES: 89-589

REMARKS: Left Revigny at 0845. First entered combat here. Set up in tents. General Patton visited.

STATION: Hincourt

DATE: 5 Nov 44

MILES: 6-595

REMARKS: Another tent set-up. Witnessed display of terrific barrage by our surrounding batteries of "240 Rifles," introducing biggest concentrated attack the Jerries ever received from our sector.

STATION: Vic-sur-Seille

DATE: 14 Nov 44

MILES: 8-603

REMARKS: Set up in shoe factory. 1st time in buildings.

STATION: Dieuze

DATE: 22 Nov 44

MILES: 10-613

REMARKS: Near RR Station. Set up tents inside of grain mill because of the impaired roof. Had to leave in a hurry. The following day the town rec'd hits from 88s!

STATION: Marimont

DATE: 23 Nov 44

MILES: 7-620

REMARKS: Set up in chateau used by German officers. Rec'd 2d visit from Gen. Patton.

STATION: Chateau Bonnefontaine

DATE: 1 Dec 44

MILES: 13-633

REMARKS: Beautiful estate, and deer hunting is apleanty!

STATION: Metz

DATE: 14 Dec 44

MILES: 62-695

REMARKS: Set up in hospital. First opportunity to visit a real city, which impressed us as very Germanic in appearance. Left here in a rush to assist in the "Ardennes Bulge."

STATION: Autelbas (Belgium)

DATE: 20 Dec 44

MILES: 72-757

REMARKS: The station was comprised half of tents, and the rest was established in the Town Hall. Had first experience with buzz bombs. Hospitality unsurpassed.

STATION: Redange (Luxembourg)

DATE: 26 Dec 44

MILES: 11-778

REMARKS: Set up in school bldgs all over town. Mickey Rooney visits station.

STATION: Grosbous

DATE: 3 Jan 45

MILES: 6-784

REMARKS: Set up in hotel, and the wards all over town. We have really hit cold weather here.

STATION: Boulaide

DATE: 22 Jan 45

MILES: 15-799

REMARKS: Admission, Surgical, Evacuation and Shock set up in field; all rest in bldgs. All over town. Had to shovel away the snow to erect tents.

STATION: Boulay (France)

DATE: 29 Jan 45

MILES: 79-878

REMARKS: Long, cold ride down into France. We are in a prison hospital. Best set-up of all. Beds, movies, steam-heat, and few patients. Start of drive for the finish.

STATION: Saarburg (Germany)

DATE: 7 Mar 45

MILES: 37-915

REMARKS: Took over for one night from the 94th, and gave it back the following day.

STATION: Beurig

DATE: 9 Mar 45

MILES: 3-918

REMARKS: Stayed in German barracks. 3rd drives to the Rhine.

STATION: Urexweiler

DATE: 20 Mar 45

MILES: 24-942

REMARKS: Tent-set up. 1st platoon left here with skeleton crew and mingled with 7th army elements in Landstuhl.

STATION: Landstuhl

DATE: 22 Mar 45

MILES: 31-973

REMARKS: Set up in German hospital. POWs all around. Bowie & Hudson here. 2d plt joins 1st here, but moves on 2 hrs after dinner.

STATION: Alzey

DATE: 23 Mar 45

MILES: 47-1020

REMARKS: Arrived late at nite; set up in beautiful bldgs., like a summer estate. 1st plt arrives in "liberated" bus just at supper time. Some men claiming ownership to abandoned VOLKSWAGONS!! 1st plt pulls out to cross Rhine under enemy air activity.

STATION: Leehaim

DATE: 25 Mar 45

MILES: 24-1044

REMARKS: 2d plt crosses Rhine here and by-passes 1st plt which is set up here in tents. First purple-heart to be given to any clearing station man is awarded to Sgt. Royal W. Harvey, who was wounded during Rhine Crossing.

STATION: Darmstadt

DATE: 26 Mar 45

MILES: 8-1052

REMARKS: Set up in Heinie barracks. Every bldg. in town demolished except two hospitals. Armor is really rolling!

STATION: Dudenhofen

DATE: 27 Mar 45

MILES: 21-1073

REMARKS: 1st plt set up in tents. Weather is bleak and cold.

STATION: Hanau

DATE: 30 Mar 45

MILES: 12-1085

REMARKS: Established in the luxurious and palatial estate of Friedrich-Wilhelm, Count von Essen. 'Twas here that the phrase "Lootin' Verbootin" was coined. Three of the boys took "bath" while canoeing in river!

STATION: Budingen

DATE: 31 Mar 45

MILES: 20-1105

REMARKS: 1st plt set up in school; 2d by-passes them at noon to keep up with infantry heading N.E.

STATION: Hosenfeld

DATE: 1 Apr 45

MILES: 30-1135

REMARKS: 2d platoon set up in tents; 1st plt cut off by Heinies. MPS captured near here. Called in tanks for security.

STATION: Fulda

DATE: 3 Apr 45

MILES: 13-1148

REMARKS: More Heinie barracks! These, however, were intact. Remained overnight and moved on following AM

STATION: Geisa

DATE: 4 Apr 45

MILES: 19-1167

REMARKS: Set up in an art school. (Had to evict the English speaking family.) Weather: Chilly.

STATION: Wasungen

DATE: 6 Apr 45

MILES: 27-1194

REMARKS: Set up in school. First showers in 2 wks. Every one going to Zella-Mehlis for P-38s. UPS moves up with us and Hdqts. (Hitherto they have been too far in the unprotected rear.)

STATION: Suhl

DATE: 8 April 45

MILES: 21-1215

REMARKS: Established in a large <u>Oberschule</u> (High School) Air rifle and Schmausier factory just across street. Every one is getting parts for 7.65s and assembling same.

STATION: Sachsendorf

DATE: 12 April 45

MILES: 27-1242

REMARKS: 1st plt established in tavern. Personnel go to school again! News of FDR's death announced this evening. 2nd plt by-passes without stopping. Kitchen set up in barn in rear of tavern.

STATION: Sonneburg

DATE: 13 Apr 45

MILES: 22-1264

REMARKS: Set up in an art school. (Had to evict the English speaking family.) Weather: Chilly.

STATION: Helmsbrecht

DATE: 15 Apr 45

MILES: 38-1302

REMARKS: Station opens in <u>another</u> school! 1st plt raids tavern; beer flows freely!! The Burgemeister's attempt at suicide proved successful the following morning.

STATION: Kemnath

DATE: 20 Apr 45

MILES: 47-1349

REMARKS: Traveled the famed <u>Reichsautobahn</u>. Saw Beyreuth, home of Richard Wagner. Set up in a parochial school. Heading south again along the Czechoslovakian border.

STATION: Grafenwohr

DATE: 22 Apr 45

MILES: 12-1361

REMARKS: 1st platoon set up in Heinie barracks. Some of the boys review their equestrian skill. Supurb mess hall. 2d missed out on chicken dinner, for they by-passed at noon!!

STATION: Schwarzenfeld

DATE: 23 Apr 45

MILES: 45-1406

REMARKS: Picked up Hungarian prisinors enroute. Roads filled with Russian, Czech, and Polish soldier-refugees. Set-up in Madchenschule. (Girl's school) Saw <u>more</u> German atrocities. Townsfolks forded to build coffins for these dead; bury them and display the black flag of mourning for 30 days

STATION: Falkenstein

DATE: 25 Apr 45

MILES: 41-1447

REMARKS: 1st plt set up in a bar-room. 2d plt by-passes at noon. Entering very hilly country.

STATION: Hitterfels

DATE: 26 Apr 45

MILES: 62-1509

REMARKS: Set up in bldgs and tents. Planes strafing and ack-ack banging over our heads late this evening.

STATION: Egg

DATE: 27 Apr 45

MILES: 22-1531

REMARKS: 1st platoon set up in tents. 2d plt moves in on following day and sets up in a neighboring dairy farm. Had fresh butter and milk.

STATION: Zenting

DATE: 29 Apr 45

MILES: 27-1558

REMARKS: 2d platoon establishes itself on a hillside. We "liberated" (!) all-ready out firewood from the village. First view of "The Beautiful Blue Danube" this afternoon. Late this evening the German radio announced the death of Reichsfuhrer Adolf Hitler.

STATION: Tittling

DATE: 30 Apr 45

MILES: 10-1568

REMARKS: 1st plt set up in a <u>Gasthaus</u>. (Hotel) Cold & Rainy. (Snow flurries in AM!) Town badly battered by artillery fire.

STATION: Hauzenberg

DATE: 1 May 45

MILES: 23-1591

REMARKS: 2d plt set up in a gym; kitchen in tents; men sleeping in bar-room.

STATION: Hauzenberg

DATE: 3 May 45

MILES: 23-1591

REMARKS: 1st plt moves in and is assigned quarters in a <u>Gasthaus</u> several blocks from the Clearing Station.

STATION: Putzleindorf (Austria)

DATE: 4 May 45

MILES: 31-1622

REMARKS: 1st plt set up in group of private bldgs.. Tyrolian mts., more commonly known as Austrian Alps were seen in the distance as we passed thru Southern Germany and into Ostreich (Austria) this PM Ours is only front left; expect surrender soon. 2d plt moves up here on the 5th and establishes itself in a school a block away.

STATION: Aigen

DATE: 7 May 45

MILES: 26-1648

REMARKS: Set up in an ancient monastary. Word of the unconditional surrender of Germany – Hitler's "Invinceable 3rd Reich – reaches us here in Aigen. The bodies of Dr. Goebbles and his family have been found by Russians in Berlin. The G- family had taken poison! My "Aigen" back; the war is over!

<u>END</u> <u>OF</u> <u>THE</u> <u>LINE</u>

S/Sgt Cooper

"MEMOIRS"

An abridgement of the travels of the 114th Medical Battalion
Clearing Company in combat from 7 September 1944 to VE Day,
the 8th of May, 1945.
§-§

STATION	DATE	MILES	REMARKS
Videcosville, (France)	7 Sept 44	19	Arrived Cherbourg France at 10:00 A.M. Disembarked at 1130 Traveled by truck 15 miles to starting point. Hiked a LONG 4 miles --in the rain-- to bivouac area in Videcos- ville. "A Salute to Videcosville, whose motto is: 'Mines Cleared to Hedges'"!
Videcosville	15 Sept 44		10 of our truck drivers trfd to 263rd FA Bn to serve as driv- ers on the "Red Ball Highway." Daily class in French.
Carteret (Les Moitiers d'Allonne)	27 Sept 44	27-46	Station established in tents in field over- looking bay. Boys have first sample of the Normandy Special: Cal- vados and cidre! Rumors: Elements of YD committed on 3rd Army front
Le Mans	18 Oct 44	172-218	Left Carteret biv- ouac area at 0015. Traveled 172 miles to vicinity of Le Mans.
Longjumeau	19 Oct 44	120-386	Left Le Mans 0920. Traveled 120 miles, and bivouaced on a famed race track near Paris.
Revigny	20 Oct 44	162-500	Left Longjumeau at 0830. Bartered for cidre along the way.
Cerneuil (Vicinity of Nancy)	21 Oct 44	89-589	Left Revigny at 0845. First entered combat here. Set up in tents. General Patton visited.
Hincourt	5 Nov 44	6-595	Another tent set-up. Witnessed display of terrific barrage by our surrounding batteries of "240 Rifles," intro- ducing biggest concen- trated bombardment the Jerries ever received from our sec- tor.
Vic-sur-Seille	14 Nov 44	8-603	Set up in shoe factory, 1st time in buildings.

M E M O I R S

STATION	DATE	MILES	REMARKS
Dieuze	22 Nov 44	10-615	Near RR Station. Set up tents inside of grain mill because of the impaired roof. Had to leave in a hurry. The following day the town rec'd hits from 88s!
Harimont	23 Nov 44	7-620	Set up in chateau used by German officers. Rec'd 2d visit from Gen. Patton
Chateau Bonnefontaine	1 Dec 44	13-633	Beautiful estate, and deer hunting is aplenty!
			CROWN REGENTS WE HERE___ DUE TO PHYSICAL AILMENTS.
Metz	14 Dec 44	62-695	Set up in hospital. First opportunity to visit a real city, which impressed us as very Germanic in appearance. Left here in a rush to assist in the "Ardennes Bulge."
Autelbas (Belgium)	20 Dec 44	72-767	The station was comprised half of tents, and the rest was established in the Town Hall. Had first experience with buzz bombs. Hospitality unsurpassed.
Redange (Luxembourg)	26 Dec 44	11-778	Set up in school bldgs all over town. Mickey Rooney visits station.
Grosbous	3 Jan 45	6-784	Set up in hotel, and the wards all over town. We have really hit cold weather here.
Soulaide	22 Jan 45	15-799	Admission, Surgical, Evacuation and Shock set up in field; all rest in bldgs all over town. Had to shovel away the snow to erect tents.
Boulay (France)	29 Jan 45	79-878	Long, cold ride down into France. We are in a prison hospital. Best set-up of all. Beds, movies, steam-heat, and for patients. Start of drive for the finish
Saarburg (Germany)	7 Mar 45	37-915	Took over for one night from the 96th, and gave it back the following day.
Beurig	9 Mar 45	3-918	Stayed in German barracks. 3rd drives to the Rhine.
			REIMSBACH ERRONEOUSLY OMITTED. 16 MAR.
Urexweiler	20 Mar 45	24-942	Tent-set up. 1st platoon left here with skeleton crew and mingled with 7th army elements in Landstuhl.

STATION	DATE	MILES	REMARKS
Landstuhl	22 Mar 45	31-973	Set up in German hospital. POWs all around. Bowie & Hudson ▓▓▓▓▓ here. 2d plt joins 1st here, but moves on 2 hrs after dinner.
Alzey	23 Mar 45	47-1020	Arrived late at nite; set up in beautiful bldgs., like a summer estate. 1st plt arrives in "liberated" bus just at supper time. Some men claiming owner-ship to abandoned VOLKS-WAGONS!! 1st plt pulls out to cross Rhine under enemy air activity.
Lecheim	25 Mar 45	24-104"	2d plt crosses Rhine here and by-passes 1st plt which is set up here in tents. First purple-heart to be given to any clear-ing station man is awarded to Sgt. Royal W. Harvey, who was wounded during Rhine Crossing.
Darmstadt	26 Mar 45	8-1052	Set up in Heinie barracks. Every bldg in town demolished except two hospitals. Armor is really rolling!
Dudenhofen	27 Mar 45	21-1073	1st plt set up in tents. Weather is bleak and cold.
Hanau	30 Mar 45	12-1085	Established in the luxurious and palatial estate of Friedrich-Wilhelm, Count von Essen. 'Twas here that the phrase "Lootin' Verbootin" was coined. Three of the boys took bath while canoeing in river!
Budingen	31 Mar 45	20-1105	1st plt set up in school; 2d by-passes them at noon to keep up with infantry heading N.E.
Hosenfeld	1 Apr 45	30-1135	2d platoon set up in tents; 1st plt cut off by Heinies. MPs captured near here. Called in tanks for security.
Fulda	3 Apr 45	13-1148	More Heinie barracks! These, however, were in-tact. Remained overnight and moved on following AM
Geisa	4 Apr 45	19-1167	Set up in an art school. (Had to evict the English speaking family.) Weather: Chilly.
Wasungen	6 Apr 45	27-1194	Set-up in school. First showers in 2 wks. Every one going to Zella-Mehlis for P-38s. UPS moves up with us and Hdqts. (Hitherto they have been too far in the unprotected rear.)

STATION	DATE	MILES	REMARKS
Suhl	8 April 45	21-1215	Established in a large Oberschule (High School). Air rifle and Schmauser factory just across street. Every one is getting parts for 7.65s and assembling same.
Sachsendorf	12 April 45	27-1242	1st plt established in tavern. Personnel go to school again! News of FDR's death announced this evening. 2d plt by-passes without stopping. Kitchen set up in barn in rear of tavern.
Sonneburg	13 Apr 45	22-1264	Set up in a hospital insurance bldg. The city, which was afire when we entered, still smoldered upon our departure.
Helmsbrecht	15 Apr 45	38-1302	Station opens in another school! 1st plt finds tavern; beer flows freely!! The Burgomeister's attempt at suicide proved successfull the following morning.
Kemnath	20 Apr 45	47-1349	Traveled the famed Reichsautobahn. Saw Bey-ruth, home of Richard Wagner. Set up in a parochial school. Heading south again along the Czechoslovakian border.
Grafenwohr	22 Apr 45	12-1361	1st platoon set up in Heinle barracks. Some of the boys review their equestrian skill. Superb mess hall. 2d missed out on chicken dinner, for they by-passed at noon!!
Schwarzenfeld	23 Apr 45	45-1406	Picked up Hungarian prisoners enroute. Roads filled with Russian, Czech, and Polish soldier-refugees. Set-up in Madchenschule. (Girls' school) Saw more German atrocities. Townsfolks forced to build coffins for these dead; bury them and display the black flag of mourning for 30 days
Falkenstein	25 Apr 45	41-1447	1st plt set up in a bar-room. 2d plt by-passes at noon. Entering very hilly country.
Mitterfels	26 Apr 45	62-1509	Set up in bldgs and tents. Planes strafing and ack-ack banging over our heads late this evening.

STATION	DATE	MILES	REMARKS
Eging	27 Apr 45	22-1531	1st platoon set up in tents, 2d plt moves in on following day and sets up in a neighboring dairy farm. Had fresh butter and milk.
Zenting	29 Apr 45	27-1558	2d platoon establishes itself on a hillside. We "liberated" (!) all-ready cut firewood from the village. First view of "The Beautiful Blue Danube" this afternoon. Late this evening the German radio announced the death of Reichsführer Adolf Hitler.
Tittling	30 Apr 45	10-1568	1st plt set up in a Gasthaus. (Hotel) Cold & Rainy. (Snow flurries in Alps) Town badly battered by artillery fire.
Hauzenburg	1 May 45	23-1591	2d plt set up in a gym; kitchen in tents; men sleeping in bar-room.
	3 May 45		1st plt moves in and is assigned quarters in a Gasthaus several blocks from the Clearing Station.
Putzleinsdorf (Austria)	4 May 45	31-1622	1st plt set up in group of private bldgs. Tyrolian mts., more commonly known as Austrian Alps were seen in the distance as we passed thru Southern Germany and into Östreich (Austria) this PM. Ours is only front left; expect surrender soon. 2d plt moves up here on the 5th and establishes itself in a school a block away.
Aigen	7 May 45	26-1648	Set up in an ancient monastery. Word of the unconditional surrender of Germany --Hitler's "Invincible 3rd Reich-- reaches us here in Aigen. The bodies of Dr. Goebbles and his family have been found by Russians in Berlin. The G- family had taken poison! By "Aigen" back; the war is over!

END OF THE LINE

oOo
--o--
oOo

Note: According to Tf + E we were allowed 5% for typographical errors + misspelled words.
JW.

APPENDIX B: Scientific Studies

1) ANDREA DANESE M.D., Ph.D; Clinical Lecturer in Child & Adolescent Psychiatry; Kings College London, University of London et al.

Childhood maltreatment predicts adult inflammation in a life-course study

Andrea Danese*, Carmine M. Pariante†, Avshalom Caspi*‡§, Alan Taylor*, and Richie Poulton¶

*Medical Research Council Social, Genetic, and Developmental Psychiatry Centre and †Department of Psychological Medicine, Institute of Psychiatry, King's College London, London SE5 8AF, United Kingdom; ‡Department of Psychology and Neuroscience, Psychiatry, and Behavioral Science, and Institute of Genome Sciences and Policy, Duke University, Durham, NC 27708-0086; and ¶Dunedin School of Medicine, University of Otago, Dunedin 9015, New Zealand

Communicated by Burton H. Singer, Princeton University, Princeton, NJ, November 30, 2006 (received for review September 20, 2006)

Stress in early life has been associated with insufficient glucocorticoid signaling in adulthood, possibly affecting inflammation processes. Childhood maltreatment has been linked to increased risk of adult disease with potential inflammatory origin. However, the impact of early life stress on adult inflammation is not known in humans. We tested the life-course association between childhood maltreatment and adult inflammation in a birth cohort followed to age 32 years as part of the Dunedin Multidisciplinary Health and Development Study. Regression models were used to estimate the effect of maltreatment on inflammation, adjusting for co-occurring risk factors and potential mediating variables. Maltreated children showed a significant and graded increase in the risk for clinically relevant C-reactive protein levels 20 years later, in adulthood [risk ratio (RR) = 1.80, 95% confidence interval (CI) = 1.26–2.58]. The effect of childhood maltreatment on adult inflammation was independent of the influence of co-occurring early life risks (RR = 1.56, 95% CI = 1.08–2.31), stress in adulthood (RR = 1.64, 95% CI = 1.12–2.39), and adult health and health behavior (RR = 1.76, 95% CI = 1.23–2.51). More than 10% of cases of low-grade inflammation in the population, as indexed by high C-reactive protein, may be attributable to childhood maltreatment. The association between maltreatment and adult inflammation also generalizes to fibrinogen and white blood cell count. Childhood maltreatment is a previously undescribed, independent, and preventable risk factor for inflammation in adulthood. Inflammation may be an important developmental mediator linking adverse experiences in early life to poor adult health.

C-reactive protein | development | epidemiology | risk factor | stress

Inflammation is an integral part of the stress response (1–3). In the context of the "fight or flight" reaction, acute psychosocial stress can induce activation of the transcription nuclear factor κB and secretion of proinflammatory cytokines, presumably by adrenergic stimulation (4, 5). These are chief stimulators of acute-phase proteins, such as C-reactive protein, which promote resistance to infection and repair of damaged tissues. Through the production of proinflammatory cytokines, immune activation progressively stimulates the secretion of glucocorticoids, and glucocorticoid signaling, in turn, terminates the inflammatory response once the threat fades (1).

Early life adverse experiences may disrupt the potentially adaptive response to stress. Animal models suggest that maternal care exerts a critical influence on the development of the stress response (6) and may alter the long-term predisposition to inflammation (7). In humans, adults who reported experiences of childhood maltreatment showed a reduced ability of glucocorticoid signaling to control the hypothalamic-pituitary-adrenal axis in response to a psychosocial stress test (8). Given the inhibitory influence of glucocorticoids on inflammation, this finding suggests that maltreated children also might show increased levels of inflammation in adulthood.

Also, adults who were abused as children have been shown to be at increased risk of disease with potential inflammatory origin (9, 10). However, the impact of early life stress on inflammation has not been investigated in humans to date. The persistent activation of inflammatory pathways could be one of the mechanisms through which early life adverse experiences alter long-term health outcomes.

Our first aim was to test the hypothesis that maltreated children are characterized by an increased risk of clinically relevant high sensitivity C-reactive protein (hsCRP) levels in adulthood. We chose hsCRP because it is thought to be one of the most reliable indicators of inflammation and recently has been endorsed as an adjunct to traditional risk factor screening for cardiovascular disease by the Centers for Disease Control and Prevention and the American Heart Association (11).

Our second aim was to test whether childhood maltreatment was an independent risk factor for adult inflammation. We tested three alternative explanations for this life-course association. According to the "co-occurring risk hypothesis," maltreated children may experience other early life risks (12) that could be responsible for inflammation in adulthood. We measured three potential early life risks, low birth weight (13), socioeconomic disadvantage (14), and low intelligence quotient (IQ) (15), and tested whether maltreatment still predicted adult inflammation after controlling for co-occurring risks. According to the "adult stress hypothesis," maltreated children grow up to be exposed to more stress (12). We measured three indicators of stress that have been linked to inflammation, low status attainment (16), depression (17), and perceived stress (18), and tested whether childhood maltreatment is related to adult inflammation because maltreated children experience more stressful lives when they grow up. According to the "health-behavior hypothesis," maltreated children may engage in more health-damaging behaviors and show poorer health in adulthood, factors that have been independently associated with inflammation (19, 20). We measured indicators of the metabolic syndrome, smoking, physical activity, and diet, and tested whether the association between childhood maltreatment and adult inflammation is accounted for by these factors. If childhood maltreatment is an independent risk factor, its association with adult inflammation should still be significant after controlling for these confounding effects.

Our third aim was to extend this inquiry to fibrinogen and white blood cells (WBCs), two other common markers of inflammation that also show significant association with cardiovascular disease (21). We tested whether the association between childhood maltreatment and adult inflammation was specific to

Author contributions: A.D., C.M.P., A.C., and R.P. designed research; A.D., C.M.P., A.C., and R.P. performed research; A.D., A.C., and A.T. analyzed data; and A.D., C.M.P., A.C., A.T., and R.P. wrote the paper.

The authors declare no conflict of interest.

Abbreviations: CI, confidence interval; hsCRP, high sensitivity C-reactive protein; IQ, intelligence quotient; RR, risk ratio; SES, socioeconomic status.

§To whom correspondence should be addressed. E-mail: a.caspi@iop.kcl.ac.uk.

This article contains supporting information online at www.pnas.org/cgi/content/full/0610362104/DC1.

© 2007 by The National Academy of Sciences of the USA

Table 1. The association of childhood maltreatment with biomarkers and risk factors

Risk factor	Level	Maltreatment, % (n)*			P value[†]
		No	Probable	Definite	
		64 (551)	27 (232)	9 (83)	
Adult inflammation:					
hsCRP (>3 mg/liter), % (n)		18 (99)	21.3 (49)	32.5 (27)	0.011
hsCRP, (log) mean (SE)		0.16 (0.047)	0.24 (0.074)	0.51 (0.148)	0.028
Fibrinogen, mean (SE)		2.55 (0.025)	2.61 (0.036)	2.72 (0.068)	0.035
WBC, mean (SE)		7.39 (0.071)	7.93 (0.124)	8.08 (0.221)	<0.0001
Co-occurring early life risks:					
Low birth weight, % (n)		5.1 (28)	3.0 (7)	7.2 (6)	0.222
Child SES, % (n)	Low	14.7 (81)	25.3 (58)	37.8 (31)	
	Medium	67.8 (373)	60.3 (138)	48.8 (40)	
	High	17.5 (96)	14.4 (33)	13.4 (11)	<0.0001
Low child IQ, % (n)		8.8 (47)	20.0 (46)	22.0 (18)	<0.0001
Adult stress indicators:					
SES, % (n)	Low	26.7 (147)	37.1 (86)	41.0 (34)	
	Medium	35.7 (196)	32.3 (75)	32.5 (27)	
	High	37.6 (207)	30.6 (71)	26.5 (22)	0.01
Major depression, % (n)		12.7 (70)	16.6 (39)	32.5 (27)	<0.0001
High perceived stress, % (n)		23.7 (129)	28.6 (66)	42.2 (35)	0.001
Adult health and health behavior:					
Cardiovascular risk cluster, % (n)		14.2 (78)	22.1 (51)	18.1 (15)	0.024
Smoking, % (n)	Nonsmoker	63.6 (350)	53.0 (123)	36.1 (30)	
	Up to 10 per day	17.3 (95)	19.4 (45)	18.1 (15)	
	11 to 20 per day	15.6 (86)	22.4 (52)	30.1 (25)	
	>20 per day	3.5 (18)	5.2 (12)	15.7 (13)	<0.0001
Physical activity, % (n)	Light	26.0 (142)	23.4 (54)	21.7 (18)	
	Moderate	26.0 (142)	24.2 (56)	21.7 (18)	
	Hard	25.1 (137)	26.0 (60)	25.3 (21)	
	Very hard	23.0 (126)	26.4 (61)	31.3 (26)	0.712
Diet (fruit, vegetable intake), % (n)	Very low	25.8 (142)	24.2 (56)	30.1 (25)	
	Low	33.8 (186)	40.3 (93)	32.5 (27)	
	High	20.6 (113)	22.1 (51)	16.9 (14)	
	Very high	19.8 (109)	13.4 (31)	20.5 (17)	0.252
Others:					
Male sex, % (n)		53.5 (295)	53.9 (125)	44.6 (37)	0.295
Use of antiinflammatory medication, % (n)		32.8 (179)	27.7 (64)	19.8 (16)	0.035

*Study members analyzed here have the same prevalence of maltreatment as the original birth cohort (no maltreatment, 64%; probable maltreatment, 27%; definite maltreatment, 9%).
[†]Association with categorical variables has been estimated with the Fisher's exact test, whereas association with continuous variables has been estimated with one-way ANOVA. Some of the cell sizes vary slightly because of missing cases.

hsCRP or more generally predicted the clustering of inflammation factors in the same individuals.

Results

Table 1 shows the biomarkers of adult inflammation as well as the risk factors associated with childhood maltreatment. The regression analysis in Table 2 (baseline model) shows that children in the definite maltreatment group were 1.80 [95% confidence interval (CI) = 1.26–2.58] times and children in the probable maltreatment group were 1.18 (95% CI = 0.87–1.60) times more likely to have elevated hsCRP in adulthood compared with nonmaltreated children. Analyses restricted to the sample of participants free from drugs with substantial effect on hsCRP, namely statins and estrogens, yielded overlapping results. Children in the definite maltreatment group were 1.86 (95% CI = 1.25–2.61) times more likely to have elevated hsCRP in adulthood compared with nonmaltreated children. We also sought to ensure that the association between maltreatment and inflammation was not simply a function of individuals having extreme hsCRP values. We excluded all individuals with hsCRP >10 mg/liter (11) and observed that children with a history of

maltreatment were still 1.59 (95% CI = 1.02–2.50) times more likely to have elevated hsCRP in adulthood compared with nonmaltreated children.

Consistent with the co-occurring risk hypothesis, maltreated children were significantly more likely than nonmaltreated children to experience co-occurring early life risks (Table 1). Although early life risks were independently associated with adult inflammation (Table 2, baseline model), even after controlling for those risks the association between maltreatment and elevated adult hsCRP remained significant, risk ratio (RR) = 1.58 (95% CI = 1.08–2.31) (Table 2, model 1).

Consistent with the adult stress hypothesis, maltreated children also were significantly more likely than nonmaltreated children to experience adult stress (Table 1). However, even after controlling for these indicators of stress, the association between childhood maltreatment and elevated adult hsCRP remained significant, RR = 1.64 (95% CI = 1.12–2.39) (Table 2, model 2).

Finally, consistent with the health-behavior hypothesis, maltreated children were more likely than nonmaltreated children to be in poor health and to engage in health-damaging behaviors

177

Table 2. The relative risk and 95% CIs from the Cox regression models with robust variance predicting high hsCRP levels (hsCRP > 3 mg/dl)

Risk factor	Level	Baseline	Model 1	Model 2	Model 3	Model 4
Childhood maltreatment:	No	1	1	1	1	1
	Probable	1.16 (0.87–1.60)	1.11 (0.81–1.52)	1.20 (0.85–1.63)	1.16 (0.86–1.56)	1.07 (0.78–1.46)
	Definite	1.82 (1.26–2.58)	1.56 (1.08–2.31)	1.64 (1.17–2.30)	1.76 (1.23–2.51)	1.61 (1.12–2.32)
Co-occurring early life risks:						
Low birth weight		1.61 (1.05–2.57)	1.34 (0.85–2.12)	—	—	1.28 (0.80–2.04)
Child SES	Low	1.56 (1.19–3.25)	1.77 (1.05–2.97)			1.47 (0.88–2.45)
	Medium	1.59 (1.00–2.52)	1.60 (1.00–2.55)			1.51 (0.95–2.40)
	High	1	1			1
Low child IQ		1.44 (1.03–2.01)	1.27 (0.91–1.78)	—	—	1.07 (0.73–1.57)
Adult stress indicators:						
SES	Low	1.36 (0.99–1.92)	—	1.23 (0.87–1.74)	—	1.16 (0.80–1.78)
	Medium	1.19 (0.85–1.67)		1.14 (0.81–1.60)		1.08 (0.78–1.51)
	High	1		1		1
Major depression		1.45 (1.06–1.99)	—	1.17 (0.83–1.64)	—	1.17 (0.83–1.64)
High perceived stress		1.45 (1.10–1.91)	—	1.22 (0.90–1.60)	—	1.17 (0.84–1.58)
Adult health and health behavior:						
CV risk cluster		2.39 (1.84–3.10)	—	—	2.50 (1.91–3.27)	2.34 (1.77–3.08)
Smoking	Nonsmoker	1	—	—	1	1
	Up to 10 per day	0.88 (0.61–1.28)			0.93 (0.64–1.35)	0.92 (0.64–1.34)
	11 to 20 per day	0.85 (0.59–1.23)			0.76 (0.52–1.10)	0.74 (0.50–1.05)
	>20 per day	1.18 (0.69–2.03)			1.14 (0.64–2.06)	1.06 (0.58–1.93)
Physical activity	Light	1.57 (1.05–2.34)	—	—	1.25 (0.83–1.88)	1.32 (0.87–1.99)
	Moderate	1.47 (0.98–2.21)			1.16 (0.78–1.73)	1.27 (0.84–1.92)
	Hard	1.30 (0.86–1.97)			1.10 (0.73–1.66)	1.13 (0.75–1.72)
	Very hard	1			1	1
Diet (fruit, vegetable) intake	Very low	1.01 (0.68–1.48)	—	—	1.09 (0.74–1.61)	1.09 (0.68–1.55)
	Low	0.78 (0.53–1.14)			0.82 (0.56–1.19)	0.81 (0.55–1.19)
	High	1.01 (0.67–1.52)			0.92 (0.60–1.38)	0.95 (0.64–1.42)
	Very high	1			1	1
Others:						
Male sex		0.50 (0.38–0.66)	0.54 (0.41–0.72)	0.54 (0.41–0.72)	0.50 (0.38–0.68)	0.56 (0.41–0.78)
Use of antiinflammatory medication		1.33 (1.01–1.75)	1.34 (1.02–1.76)	1.37 (1.03–1.81)	1.35 (1.03–1.77)	1.37 (1.03–1.82)

The baseline model shows the bivariate analysis of the association between putative risk factors and high hsCRP. Model 1 indexes the co-occurring risk hypothesis, showing the RR of high hsCRP according to maltreatment experiences adjusted for low birth weight, childhood SES, and low childhood IQ. Model 2 indexes the adult stress hypothesis, showing the RR of high hsCRP according to maltreatment experiences adjusted for adult SES, major depression, and high perceived stress. Model 3 indexes the health-behavior hypothesis, showing the RR of high hsCRP according to maltreatment experiences adjusted for cardiovascular risk cluster, smoking, physical activity, and diet. Model 4 shows the RR of high hsCRP according to maltreatment experiences adjusted for all child and adult risk factors. CI values are shown in parentheses.

(Table 1). After controlling for these factors, the association between childhood maltreatment and elevated adult hsCRP still remained significant, RR = 1.76 (95% CI = 1.23–2.51) (Table 2, model 3).

Even after controlling for all co-occurring childhood and adult risk factors simultaneously, the association between childhood maltreatment and elevated adult hsCRP remained significant, RR = 1.61 (95% CI = 1.12–2.32) (Table 2, model 4).

Under the assumptions of causality and independence, we estimated that 11.2% of the cases of high hsCRP in the general population were attributable to childhood maltreatment.

The significant dose–response association between childhood maltreatment and inflammation generalized to continuous measures of (logged) hsCRP, fibrinogen, WBCs, and the composite factor score of inflammation [Table 1, Fig. 1, and supporting information (SI) Tables 3–5].

Conclusion

This longitudinal-prospective study links exposure to childhood maltreatment in the first decade of life to specific, clinically significant biomarkers of inflammation in adulthood. In light of the role of inflammation in the pathophysiology of cardiovascular disease, diabetes, and chronic lung disease (22–24), and of

the increased risk for such disease in adults maltreated as children (9, 30), we suggest that inflammation may be an important mechanism mediating the adverse effect of early life stress on adult health.

Current evidence suggests the possibility of stress response programming by early life adverse experiences. Experimental research suggests that early life stress can induce a persistent condition of insufficient glucocorticoid signaling (6, 8). In animals, epigenetic programming seems to be responsible for the effects of early life stress on later stress reactivity, by inducing persistent, although reversible, reduction in glucocorticoid receptor gene expression (6). Insufficient glucocorticoid signaling, in turn, might lead to an unrestrained inflammatory state in adults maltreated as children, hampering the extinction of otherwise adaptive responses to stress (1, 2). Similarly, early life stressful experiences might reduce inhibitory cholinergic neurotransmission (25), favoring inflammation persistence (26).

The experimental design needed to directly test causation in humans, namely randomly assigning children to maltreatment, is not ethical. Findings from this longitudinal child-to-adult study therefore provide crucial data and appear to meet several criteria suggestive of a causal association between childhood maltreatment and adult inflammation (27). First, maltreatment preceded the

178

2) THE ACE STUDY

The Adverse Childhood Effects (ACE) Study is ongoing collaborative research between the Centers for Disease Control and Prevention in Atlanta, GA, and Kaiser Permanente in San Diego, CA

Babies who receive above-average levels of affection from their mothers are less likely to grow up to be emotionally distressed.

STORY HIGHLIGHTS

Adults who recieved above-average levels of affection were less likely to be anxious

The study followed nearly 500 infants into their 30s

The babies-turned-adults were interviewed about their levels of emotional distress

The findings make a strong case for policies that would help foster positive interactions

RELATED TOPICS

Child Development

Psychology

Parenting

Social and Behavioral Sciences

(Health.com) -- Babies whose mothers are attentive and caring tend to grow into happy, well-adjusted children. But the psychological benefits of having a doting mother may extend well beyond childhood, a new study suggests.

According to the study, which followed nearly 500 infants into their 30s, babies who receive above-average levels of affection and attention from their mothers are less likely than other babies to grow up to be emotionally distressed, anxious, or hostile adults.

Health.com: Feeling stressed? Try calling mom

What's more, the link between the emotional health of adults and their mothers' affection was evident even though the mothers and babies were observed for a single day, when the babies were just 8 months old.

"Even a simple assessment of the quality of the mother-infant interaction at such an early age captures something very important in terms of the future psychological health of that infant," says Joanna Maselko, Ph.D., the lead author of the study and an assistant professor of psychiatry and behavioral sciences at Duke University Medical School, in Durham, North Carolina.

The findings, which appear in the "Journal of Epidemiology and Community Health," make a strong case for policies that would help foster positive interactions between infants and parents, such as paid parental leave, Maselko says.

Health.com: Your secret to happiness at every age

The study also suggests that health insurance should cover services -- such as infant-massage classes -- that have been shown to strengthen the child-caregiver relationship, says Robin Gurwitch, Ph.D., a professor of developmental and behavioral pediatrics at Cincinnati Children's Hospital.

"Early experience can be a mediating factor on what happens to us as adults, and we need to look at things that we can do to improve parent-child bonding that can then perhaps serve as a protective factor later," Gurwitch says.

The study included 482 babies born in Providence in the early 1960s. Along with their mothers, the babies were part of a larger, nationwide study on pregnancy and infancy.

When the babies were eight months old, psychologists observed the mothers' interactions with them as the babies took a series of development tests. The psychologists rated the mother's affection and attention level on a five-point scale ranging from "negative" to "extravagant." The vast

180

majority of the interactions (85 percent) were considered "warm," or normal.

Health.com: Boost your mood naturally

Roughly 30 years later, the babies-turned-adults were interviewed about their levels of emotional distress. The adults whose mothers had displayed "extravagant" or "caressing" affection (the two top ratings) were much less likely than their less-doted-on peers to be anxious. They were also less likely to report hostility, distressing social interactions, and psychosomatic symptoms.

The findings add to a large body of psychological research on mother-child attachment that suggests that healthy bonds between young children and parents are crucial to a child's emotional development.

Maselko and her colleagues suspect that their findings may be explained in part by the hormone oxytocin, which acts as a brain chemical. Also known as the "bonding hormone" or "cuddle hormone," oxytocin is released during breastfeeding and other moments of closeness.

Health.com: 10 habits of healthy families

"Oxytocin adds [to] the perception of trust and support, and hence is very helpful in building social bonds," Maselko explains. "It's plausible that close parent-child bonds help support the neural development of the areas of the brain that make and use oxytocin, setting up the child for more effective social interactions and mental health in the future."

For now that's just a theory, however. As the authors note, other factors -- including genetics, a mother's stress levels, or even factors that have nothing to do with the mother -- could explain the findings.

A smaller proportion of mothers with lower socioeconomic status exhibited "extravagant" or "caressing" affection than did better-off mothers, for instance. Although the researchers controlled for socioeconomic status and other characteristics, it's possible that social and financial difficulties during childhood could play a role in adult emotional distress.

Health.com: Smiling babies make moms happy

Charles Bauer, M.D., a professor of pediatrics, ob-gyn, and psychology at the University of Miami's Miller School of Medicine, says that conclusions about the role of maternal affection on a person's future mental health based on a single day of observation at eight months old are bound to be inexact.

"There are so many intervening variables between eight months and 34 years," Bauer says. "A whole cadre of factors might lead to a more stable environment, a more stable mental health picture, a more stable individual."

Enter to win a monthly Room Makeover Giveaway from MyHomeIdeas.com

* * *

CHILDHOOD TRAUMA AND ADULT ILLNESS

Have you thought about your childhood lately? If you find yourself struggling with a medical, social, or behavioral disorder that seems to defy standard treatment, you might benefit from examining your childhood.

We now have good evidence to support the link between adverse childhood experiences and later negative health effects in adulthood. The connection between those childhood experiences and later negative health effects are underscored by the decades-long, ongoing adverse childhood experiences (ACE) study, a collaboration between the Centers for Disease Control and Prevention and Kaiser Permanente.

This collaborative study began in the mid-1980s. Dr. Vincent Felitti and his colleagues working in an obesity program in Kaiser Permanente's Department of Preventive Medicine in San Diego noted that their patients who were most successful at losing weight were the ones most likely to drop out of the program. Examination of this unexpected observation revealed that the patients had been reaping sexual, physical, and emotional protective benefits from overeating and their subsequent obesity.

This realization lead to another realization: From the patient's standpoint, obesity was not a problem but a solution. A solution to what? The ACE study soon began to supply answers by finding common adverse childhood experiences in the patients participating in the study.

To date, ten adverse experiences consisting of abuse, neglect, and household dysfunction have been identified, falling into these categories of experiences during the first 18 years of life:

Abuse

1.   Emotional
2.   Physical
3.   Sexual (by contact)

Neglect

1.   Emotional
2.   Physical

Household Dysfunction

1.   Watching mother being battered
2.   Parental separation, divorce, or loss in childhood

3.   Mental illness in household
4.   Incarcerated household member
5.   Presence of alcohol and/or substance abuse

As the ACE study progressed, the researchers noted that patients who had one adverse childhood experience in their lives were at risk for having additional adverse childhood experiences. For instance, growing up in a household where the mother was battered increased the patients' risk of having one or more adverse childhood experiences in the form of:

- Emotional abuse
- Physical abuse
- Sexual abuse
- Emotional neglect
- Physical neglect
- Parental separation or divorce
- Substance abuse
- Mental illness

Thanks to this study, we now know that approximately two-thirds of our population has an ACE score of 1 or higher. The higher the score, the more likely a person will be to:

- Smoke or abuse alcohol or drugs
- Experience unintended pregnancy, teen pregnancy, miscarriage, and stillbirth
- Be promiscuous, have sex before the age of 14, and have sexually transmitted diseases
- Have poor work performance
- Attempt suicide
- Experience depression and have a poor health-related quality of life
- Have liver disease, ischemic heart disease, diabetes, obesity, and experience other leading causes of death in the United States.
- Experience a high level of perceived stress

- Have difficulty in controlling anger
- Have an increased risk of becoming a perpetrator of relationship abuse or domestic violence

The researchers conducting the ACE study note that their findings likely reflect the accumulative neurobiological effects of early trauma and stress in a person's life. Such accumulation of stress and trauma can result in long-term changes in brain function and structures. In turn, these changes can impact adult emotional and physical responses to stress and contribute to substance abuse, sexuality and memory disturbances as well as aggression.

Adult response to childhood trauma in the form of disease and behavioral disorders can appear late in life, masking the relationship between the distant trauma and current life problems. To compound matters, such adult disease and behavioral disorders are often complex and resistant to standard biologic treatment.

The ACE Study researchers recommend an approach that addresses the early childhood trauma as well as the adult disease and distress. When treating patients with past adverse childhood events, these physicians augment standard pharmacological treatment with the use of medical interviews and autobiographical writing to explore how their patients perceive that the earlier childhood events have shaped their adult life and well-being.

Ellen Taliaferro, MD, FACEP
www.healthaftertrauma.com
www.savingcindy.com
www.ellentaliaferro.com
ellent@mac.com

Ellen H. Taliaferro, MD, FACEP, is the Project Director of the Health After Trauma project of Creekside Communications. She is an author, speaker and expert witness in the area of the medical response to intimate partner violence. In 1998, she founded the Parkland Hospital Violence Intervention and Prevention (VIP) Center in Dallas, TX, and served as its Medical Director until returning home to California in 2001. She was the co-founder and former Executive Director of Physicians for a Violence-free Society (PVS).

Dr. Taliaferro co-authored the Physicians Guide to Domestic Violence. She is the editor of the Journal of Emergency Medicine Section on Violence: Recognition, Management, and Prevention, which published a series of articles on manual strangulation in October of 2001. For that series of articles, she wrote the lead article, "Walking and Talking Victims of Strangulation. Is There a New Epidemic?"

19704849R00101

Made in the USA
Charleston, SC
07 June 2013